The Water Gardener's Handbook

OTHER GARDENING BOOKS PUBLISHED BY CROOM HELM

Growing Fuchsias
K. Jennings and V. Miller

Growing Hardy Perennials
Kenneth A. Beckett

Growing Dahlias
Philip Damp

Growing Irises
G.E. Cassidy and S. Linnegar

Growing Cyclamen
Gay Nightingale

Violets
Roy E. Coombs

Plant Hunting in Nepal
Roy Lancaster

The History of Gardens
Christopher Thacker

Slipper Orchids
Robin Graham with Ronald Roy

Growing Chrysanthemums
Harry Randall and Alan Wren

Waterlilies
Philip Swindells

Climbing Plants
Kenneth A. Beckett

1000 Decorative Plants
J.L. Krempin

Better Gardening
Robin Lane Fox

Country Enterprise
Jonathan and Heather Ffrench

The Rock Gardener's Handbook
Alan Titchmarsh

Growing Bulbs
Martyn Rix

Victorians and their Flowers
Nicolette Scourse

Growing Begonias
E. Catterall

Growing Roses
Michael Gibson

The Salad Garden
Elisabeth Arter

The Water Gardener's Handbook

Philip Swindells

CROOM HELM
London & Sydney

Croom Helm Ltd, Provident House, Burrell Row,
Beckenham, Kent BR3 1AT
Croom Helm Australia Pty Ltd,
GPO Box 5097, Sydney, NSW 2001, Australia

British Library Cataloguing in Publication Data

Swindells, Philip
    The water gardener's handbook.
    1. Water gardens
    I. Title
    635.9'674   SB423

    ISBN 0-7099-3300-2

Designed and Typeset by Columns of Reading
Printed and bound in Great Britain by
Biddles Ltd, Guildford and King's Lynn

Contents

List of Figures   vii

Introduction   1

1.   Water in the Garden   2
2.   Constructing the Pool   11
3.   Hardy Deep Water Aquatics   21
4.   Marginal Plants   41
5.   Submerged and Floating Plants   54
6.   Bog Garden and Stream   63
7.   Tender Aquatics   79
8.   Fish for the Pool   97
9.   Looking After a Water Garden   118
10.   Pests and Diseases   131

Glossary   145

Appendix I: Ready Reference Guide to
Aquatic Plants   148
    Hardy Waterlilies   148
    Pondlilies   150
    Other Deep Water Aquatics   150
    Marginal Plants   150
    Floating Aquatic Plants   153
    Submerged Aquatic Plants   153
    Bog Garden Plants   154
    Ferns for the Bog Garden   158
    Tender Aquatics — Tropical Waterlilies   158

Contents

Sacred Lotus (*Nelumbos*)   159

Other Tender Aquatics   160

Tender Submerged Aquatics   160

Appendix II: Nursery Suppliers   161

Appendix III: Useful Information   163

Calculating Capacities   163

Easy Reference Table for Rectangular Pools   163

Easy Reference Table for Circular Pools   164

Volume – Rate of Flow   164

Other Useful Information   165

Index   166

List of Figures

1.1   A Formal Pool   5
1.2   An Informal Pool   5
1.3   A Pre-formed Cascade or Waterfall   7
1.4   Fountain and Waterfall, Showing Positioning of Pump   8
1.5   A More Sophisticated Type of Fountain   8
1.6   An Example of a Gargoyle   9

2.1   Calculating the Size of Liner Required   13
2.2   Pool Construction Using a Pool Liner   14
2.3   An Example of a Pre-shaped Pool   16
2.4   Pool Construction Using Concrete   18

3.1   Waterlily Planted in Soil Covered with a Layer of Gravel   22
3.2   Preparing the Waterlily for Planting   23
3.3   Planting the Waterlily in a Heavy Loam Compost   23
3.4   Filling the Basket to Within an Inch or so of the Top   23
3.5   Covering the Compost with a Layer of Pea Shingle   23
3.6   *Nymphaea tuberosa*   24
3.7   Typical Hybrid Hardy Waterlily Ready for Planting   25
3.8   *Nymphaea* 'Firecrest'   31
3.9   *Nymphaea* 'Froebeli'   33
3.10   *Nymphaea marliacea* 'Chromatella'   36
3.11   *Nymphaea pygmea* 'Helvola'   37
3.12   *Nuphar lutea*   39
3.13   *Aponogeton distachyus*   40

4.1   Preparing Marginal Plants for Planting   41
4.2   Planting Marginal Plants in a Basket   42
4.3   A Generous Layer of Pea Gravel to Prevent Fish Stirring Up the Compost   42

4.4	*Butomus umbellatus* and *Scirpus tabernaemontani* 'Zebrinus'	43
4.5	*Caltha polypetala*	44
4.6	*Menyanthes trifoliata*	48
4.7	*Ranunculus lingua* 'Grandiflora' with *Nymphaea*	50
5.1	A Well-planted Pool	54
5.2	Submerged Oxygenating Plants Planted with Buried Lead Weights	55
5.3	Planting Oxygenating Plants	56
5.4	Placing a Basket of Oxygenating Plants in the Pool	56
5.5	*Ceratophyllum demersum*	57
5.6	*Fontinalis antipyretica*	58
5.7	*Lagarosiphon major*	59
6.1	*Hemerocallis* 'Pink Charm'	67
6.2	*Lysichitum americanum*	71
6.3	*Lysichitum camtschatense*	71
6.4	*Primula bulleyana*	73
6.5	*Primula denticulata*	74
6.6	*Primula pulverulenta*	74
6.7	*Primula viali*	76
7.1	Viviparous Propagation of Tropical Waterlilies	82
7.2	*Nymphaea* 'Pride of Winterhaven'	86
7.3	Seed Heads of *Nelumbo nucifera*	88
7.4	*Nelumbo nucifera*	90
8.1	Common Goldfish	100
8.2	Shubunkin	100
8.3	Comet	100
8.4	Fantail	101
8.5	Oranda	102
8.6	Lionhead	102
8.7	Celestial	102
8.8	Golden Orfe	103
8.9	Common Rudd	104
8.10	Green Tench	105
8.11	Features of a Fish	108
9.1	Example of a Pool Heater	120

Introduction

Water gardening is a relatively new horticultural development, but one which can be enjoyed by old and young alike. Until the advent of modern materials for pool construction it had been exclusively the preserve of the wealthy, but in recent years it has grown in popularity until now it is the fastest growing interest in home gardening. The fascination with water is universal and in a garden it can be displayed in all its moods. Bubbling and frothing down a waterfall, tumbling gently from a fountain or just at rest: a placid glassy surface which reflects all about it. The quality of water enhances the general garden scene, making a contribution in its own very special way and providing the adventurous gardener with an opportunity to grow some of the lovely aquatic and bog garden plants which would otherwise be denied him.

Few gardeners need convincing of the value of water in the garden, but it is a different medium with which to work and the potential pitfalls in successfully establishing a garden pool are many. It is hoped that this guide will smooth the path for the increasing number of gardeners who are setting out to create a water garden.

CHAPTER 1

Water in the Garden

Historical
Background

The father of English gardening, William Robinson, wrote in his classic *English Flower Garden* (1895): 'Unclean and ugly pools deface our gardens; some have a mania for artificial water, the effect of water pleasing them so well that they bring it near their houses where they cannot have its good effects. But they have instead the filth that gathers in stagnant water and its evil smell on many a lawn.' That great plant hunter and gardener, Reginald Farrer, in his *Alpine and Bog Plants* (1908) concurred: 'Advice to those about to build a water garden – DON'T.' Fortunately we now understand more about the construction and management of water gardens than either Robinson or Farrer, and are now greatly aided by the modern materials and preparations available to us.

Despite the fact that water gardening has only recently attained widespread popularity with the public, it is an art that has been practised for centuries. In tombs at Beni-Hassan, a village alongside the Nile, there are pictures of gardening scenes dating from the XIIth dynasty (3000-2500 BC). One shows gardeners bring water from a pond to give to plants growing in square, evenly spaced beds. A narrow canal leads from the beds and terminates in a pond. It is believed that it was this kind of pond that used to accommodate the white-flowering tropical waterlily *Nymphaea lotus*, for the ancient Egyptians used vast quantities of the blossoms of this species in their religious festivals. Amenhotep IV grew both *N. lotus* and *N. coerulea* in ponds surrounded by flower beds in the famous palace gardens of Ikhnaton, while Rameses III (1225 BC) was said to grow 'rushes and the Lotus . . .' and have many tanks and ponds '. . . of the Lotus flowers.'

As early as the eleventh century the Chinese were reputed to be growing the tiny white-flowered *N. tetragona* extensively. Chou Tun-I a noted author of the time writes in a much quoted passage: 'Since the opening days of the T'ang Dynasty it has been fashionable to admire the paeony, but my favourite

2

is the waterlily. How stainless it rises from its slimy bed. How modestly it reposes on the clear pool, an emblem of purity and truth. Symmetrically perfect, its subtle perfume is wafted far and wide; while there it rests in spotless state, something to be regarded from a distance, and not to be profaned by familiar approach.' Similarly in Japan, waterlilies were afforded great respect and grown along with a variety of reeds and rushes in pools that were made in the shape of animals or birds with a high bank towards the back which was planted with gnarled dwarf conifers intended to be reflected in the water below.

In Greece during Homeric times grotto-like structures called nymphaeums were fashionable. However, it is unlikely that waterlilies or any other aquatic plants were grown in them as they were surrounded by trees and had constantly moving water. In Britain water gardening did not receive any attention until the early 1700s. Phillip Miller in his *Gardener's Dictionary* (1731) writes: 'In some gardens I have seen plants (waterlilies) cultivated in large troughs of water where they flourish well and annually produce great quantities of flowers.' It was not until 1849 that the general public were made aware of the great potential of aquatic plants when Joseph Paxton, gardener to the Duke of Devonshire, succeeded in flowering the giant *Victoria amazonica* for the first time and presented a flower and leaf to the Queen amidst a blaze of publicity. The development of the hardy waterlilies from the vigorous and sparsely flowered whites and yellows of the period to the bright array of colours developed later by that great French hybridist Joseph Bory Latour-Marliac fired the imagination of the gardening public and water gardening as a facet of decorative horticulture became established. Under the skilful direction of George Pring of the Missouri Botanical Garden tropical waterlilies were improved and developed so that now there is a wonderful selection of varieties in every shape, size and colour imaginable.

Siting the Water Garden

The position which a pool and associated bog garden occupies is probably the most important factor affecting the ultimate success of a water feature. Not only in a practical sense, but visually, for if one looks at any natural landscape, water will be seen at the lowest point. Only rarely in mountainous terrain is it discovered above the valley floor, and then only if trapped, where it looks ill at ease, as if impatient to tumble and cascade to a lower level. So in the garden it is important that the pool occupies a site towards the lowest point, or if this cannot be contrived, that the appearance is given that it is below the surrounding ground by carefully distributing the spoil to create such an illusion.

Few sites are perfect, and while it may be desirable to have the pool in a particular position from the visual point of view, one must consider the practical aspects. For a water garden to be successful the plants must flourish and the fish and other livestock must be content. So an open position with full uninterrupted sunlight is required, despite the fact that this encourages water-discolouring algae too. Given such a situation the pool plants will flourish and compete with the algae, the submerged oxygenating plants competing for the dissolved minerals in the water and the floating subjects reducing the light beneath the surface and therefore making life intolerable for any primitive forms of plant life that try to dwell there. Prolific plant growth on the surface of the water also provides a refuge from the midday sun for goldfish and an abundance of submerged growth ensures that there are favourable conditions in which the fish will spawn.

Sunlight is vital if fish and plants are to prosper, and while it might not be possible to provide a site without any shade at all, minimal shade should be a prime consideration. Of course shade can be created in a number of ways, and while buildings and fences are a nuisance when they cast shadows, they are not as troublesome as overhanging trees. It is the latter which present the pool owner with the greatest problem, for all have leaves which are to some extent toxic if they fall into the water and start to decompose. Not only in the autumn are they troublesome, but often during the growing period, especially those of the weeping willow, a particularly common tree for poolside planting. Although looking attractive, the weeping willow is particularly undesirable, for its foliage contains a chemical akin to aspirin, which even in small quantities is toxic to goldfish. Pendulous cherries are often used as a replacement because they are of smaller proportions and more in keeping with the average garden pool; however, they are rather unsportingly the overwintering host of the waterlily aphis. Weeping trees cannot be recommended for poolside planting at all. Only when used on a grand scale beside river or lake do they have anything to offer. The image created by W.H. Davies in his immortal lines 'A lonely pool, and let a tree, Sigh with her bosom over me' finds no place in the practical garden. Sadly shade and falling leaves are not conducive to a healthy balanced pool.

The shape, size and design which one decides upon is purely a matter of personal taste, but for the end result to be really pleasing the choice should conform to certain basic principles.

Choosing a Pool Design

Figure 1.1: A formal pool

Figure 1.2: An informal pool

For example, in a formal garden the design should be symmetrical. A circle, oval, square, rectangle or an equally balanced combination of two or three of these is desirable and any fountain or ornament that is added placed in such a position that when viewed from any angle the effect is one of equilibrium. The lines created by the pool should be clear and definite and the materials used consistent throughout. A formal pool can be raised, sunk or built against a wall without offending nature, but planting must be considered carefully for a cluttered margin or crowded water surface give a messy appearance. For a formal pool to display its beauty to the fullest extent it should be placed in a position with the full play of sunshine upon a surface only briefly punctuated by decorative planting. In many cases a formal pool that is left unplanted except for the all essential submerged oxygenating plants and maybe a solitary clump of rushes will be far more effective than one of bright blossoms and tangled foliage.

Conversely, when dealing with an informal pool, planting can be bold and in drifts which extend to the poolside and tumble into the water. Nature abhors a straight line, and so the pool should be designed on a mathematical basis with sweeping curves and arcs with definite radii. Severe and eccentric lines and contortions are the invention of man and should not find a place in the informal pool. The immediate surroundings of an informal pool, unlike those of a formal design should not be conspicuous; the harshness of the concrete or fibreglass being disguised with creeping plants like rupturewort and creeping jenny. When a rock garden is an integral part of the scheme, the rocks can be brought right down to the water's edge and even extend into the pool.

Moving Water

Moving water creates another dimension in the garden, that of sound. The soft tinkling of droplets from a fountain or the rushing and tumbling of water from a cascade adds immeasurably to the pleasure that can be derived from a garden pool. Apart from its obvious visual qualities it is invaluable in oxygenating the water, cooling it too and providing endless enjoyment for lively fish, like the golden orfe, on sultry summer days. Unfortunately few aquatic plants enjoy turbulent water, most naturally being the inhabitants of pools and quiet backwaters, so great care must be taken in the siting of a water feature if it is not to interfere with the balance of the pool.

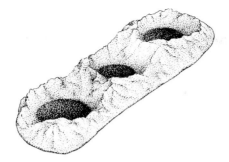

Figure 1.3: A pre-
formed cascade or
waterfall

There are a wide variety of cascade units available at present in shapes, sizes and colours to suit every taste. Some are like an irregularly shaped bowl with a lip over which the water trickles, while others come in sections of varying lengths and shapes and can be joined together to form quite complex arrangements. Installation consists of ensuring that they are assembled on a firm level base, the delivery hose being inserted in the uppermost one. Concrete cascades can be constructed by the handy gardener, and where these are well done they are probably the most attractive and serviceable.

Fountains can usually be accommodated with waterfalls by means of a two-way junction, providing that the lift required for the cascade unit is not excessive. It is very important that the pump selected should do the job properly: there is nothing worse than a lack of water volume in either a fountain or waterfall. Site the pump at the bottom of the lowest part of the pool; it is run off the mains using an ordinary waterproof cable. Either a waterfall or fountain alone is a better proposition. A fountain can be particularly pleasing, for by the judicious use of jets with different numbers and arrangements of holes, some quite pleasing spray patterns can be obtained.

In addition to traditional fountains ornaments depicting cherubs, mermaids and other mythical creatures can be purchased, each designed to take a pump outlet so that water can spout from their mouths or any object that they may be holding. One of the most attractive variations of the traditional fountain that I have seen is with different-sized bowls. Water is pumped up a tall central stem and falls into a series of bowls: the first one is quite small, but those beneath are of increasing diameter. The water from the fountain fills the first one which overflows into the second, then into the third and so on until it reaches the pool. This creates a spectacular effect, the water tumbling evenly from around each bowl and creating

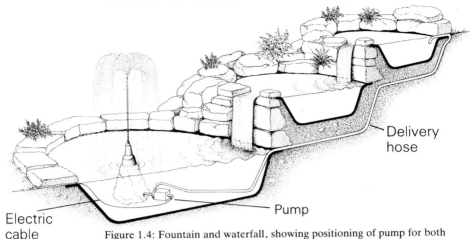

Delivery
hose

Electric
cable

Pump

Figure 1.4: Fountain and waterfall, showing positioning of pump for both features. Either a fountain or a waterfall is a better proposition, to avoid excessive water turbulence

a thin swaying curtain which turns into a bright kaleidoscope of colour on sunny days. The problem that such a feature creates is turbulence which effectively excludes the most desirable aquatic plants from the pool. However, this undesirable movement of water can be arrested to some extent by placing a large ring around the area of spread of the spray and this should create sufficient calm outside it to be able to grow a wide range of aquatic plants.

Figure 1.5: A more sophisticated type of fountain

8

Where space is restricted and there is insufficient room to accommodate a waterfall or fountain, 'masks' and gargoyles can be used. These are imitation lead or stone ornaments depicting the faces of animals or mythical characters and are flat on one side to enable them to be fastened to a wall. Water is pumped up into the mask and spouts out of the mouth into the pool below. Again water turbulence presents a problem when plants are required in the pool. If bubbling water is the main requirement and plants are not essential, then a pebble fountain can be constructed. To make one of these a small concrete chamber must be constructed to hold a reasonable amount of water and a submersible pump. A framework of iron rods is laid across the opening and supports fine mesh wire netting. A layer of well washed pebbles is placed over this and the outlet of the pump situated so that it is at the surface of the stones. Water is then able to bubble up through the pebbles. Care must be taken with this feature, however, that the chamber never becomes empty owing to evaporation.

Figure 1.6: An example of a gargoyle or 'mask'

Gardeners with plenty of room, enterprise and a love of waterfalls can do something quite spectacular by utilising ordinary building materials to create a water staircase. This was a popular feature a couple of hundred years ago in both Italian and French gardens, where water was allowed to tumble and cascade down a long row of broad steps. In the average garden one should not get over-ambitious, but it is quite possible to make an effective water staircase using sizeable concrete drainage pipes set in a bed of concrete; each pipe slightly above and behind the other. The hollow ends of the pipes are filled with concrete and then disguised with soil and plants. If the pipes are new and have not had an opportunity to weather, give them treatment with a sealant to ensure that the harmful free-lime in the cement is not washed into the pool below. Ordinary glazed drainpipes can be used, but look drab and unnatural. To complete a water staircase, all that is required is for the hosepipe from the pump outlet to be taken to the uppermost pipe.

All these features utilising moving water can be greatly enhanced by the use of underwater lighting. This can be purchased in colours which vary from red, green and blue, to white and yellow and is perfectly safe if installed by experts. The careful positioning of spotlights to highlight fountains, waterfalls, or just the cool glassy stillness of the pool's surface, will transform the garden in the early evening into a cavalcade of bright sparkling colour that the pool owner will find difficult to believe is his very own.

Chapter 2

Constructing the Pool

Modern materials have taken much of the hard work out of pool construction. Gone are the days of puddled clay and gault, when the excavation was carefully lined with soot to prevent earthworms from poking holes through the carefully laid finish, and hosepipes were kept at the ready on warm summer days in order to spray the exposed walls of the pool near ground level to prevent cracking. However, it would be less than truthful to say that building a pool is a simple matter, for much care and hard work is necessary to bring its construction to a successful conclusion. Even with all the modern materials that are available to the gardener today, the hole still has to be excavated by hand.

Types of Pool Liner

There are several different methods of pool construction to consider. Pool liners are currently the most popular as they are reasonably cheap and will suit any fanciful shape the gardener may care to design. A pool liner consists simply of a sheet of heavy gauge polythene or rubber material which is placed in the excavation and moulded to its contours by the weight of water within, finally being secured by rocks or paving slabs placed around the top.

Selecting a suitable liner presents the newcomer to water gardening with something of a dilemma, for he will see that prices vary widely for products which appear to be very similar.

Those in the lower price range are usually of 500 gauge in a sky-blue colour and made in three or four standard sizes. Mass production of liners like these makes for cheapness and, coupled with the relative ease of present day polythene manufacture, makes a popular and fast selling product. These cannot be unreservedly recommended though, if any degree of

Pool Liner
Construction

permanency is required. While it is true that with great care a pool made from this material will last for upwards of ten years, it is much more likely that it will bleach and perish between water level and ground level within three or four years. This is usually seen as cracking, and sometimes disintegration of the liner, between ground level and the water surface, effectively separating the lower part of the liner from that which is trapped beneath the paving. The most useful purpose to which this kind of liner can be put is as a small hospital pool for sick fish, or temporary accommodation for plants and fish while the main pool is being cleaned out.

The pool liners which occupy the medium price range are often the best buy for the home gardener as they are durable enough to incorporate as a permanent feature, and yet sufficiently inexpensive to be within the financial reach of almost everyone. They are invariably made from polyvinyl chloride (PVC) and available in stone, blue, green or imitation pebble, and whilst many are distributed in standard sizes, for a few extra pence it is often possible to have such a liner cut to size in accordance with the customer's wishes. Stone and blue are the most popular colours, although reversible liners giving a choice of colour are currently being manufactured.

Reinforced PVC and rubber liners occupy the more expensive class, and while being a greater outlay they do offer much better durability. The rubber kinds invariably have a black matt finish, but can be painted with a specially prepared paint of blue, stone or green. The quality PVC types on the other hand are marginally cheaper than the rubber kinds, differing principally in the presence of a terylene 'web' which gives the material much greater durability. Although visible, this does not detract from the overall appearance.

Calculating the Size of a Pool Liner

Having come to a decision over the type of liner to use, it is then necessary to calculate the size. This is done by measuring the length and breadth of the pool or, if it is of an irregular shape, the size of rectangle that will enclose the whole, and then adding on each side the measurement of the deepest part of the pool and the length required to mould into any marginal shelves that are anticipated. A further 9 in (23 cm) or a foot (30 cm) should then be added to each side to allow for anchoring at the top.

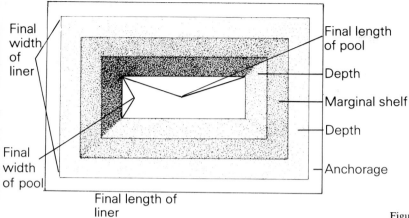

Final width of liner

Final length of pool

Depth

Marginal shelf

Depth

Anchorage

Final width of pool

Final length of liner

Figure 2.1:
Calculating the size
of liner required
(not to scale)

Excavating the Pool Shape

Before digging the hole it is a good idea to make a mock-up of the finished pool shape. This can be done by taking a length of rope or hosepipe and arranging it on the site in the desired outline. Thus the surface area and shape can be ascertained accurately. Never start excavating with just a vague idea of how the finished pool will appear, for not only may the pool liner turn out to be of the wrong dimensions, but the overall shape of the pool will quite likely not conform with its surroundings. Also be sure to allow sufficient depth for each kind of plant. Deeper areas of a foot (30 cm) to 2½ ft (75 cm) will accommodate various deep water aquatics satisfactorily, but accommodation must also be provided for marginal subjects. These prefer to grow on shallow shelves 6 or 8 in (15 or 20 cm) deep, and wide enough to take a small container.

The digging completed, the hole must be scoured for any sharp objects, such as stones or sticks, that may puncture the liner. In gravelly soils or those where flints are plentiful, it is a good idea to place a layer of sand over the pool floor to act as a cushion. The walls can be lined with thick wads of dampened newspaper to prevent any projections from ruining the liner.

Figure 2.2: Pool
construction using a
pool liner

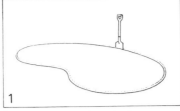

Lay out a rope or hose to the
required shape and size of the pool
adjusting until all aspects are
satisfactory. Cut out the outline of
the pool and dispense with the rope.
Always cut inside to allow for final
trimming.

Cut the sides with an inward slope
3 in (8 cm) in for every 9 in
(23 cm) down. A marginal shelf
should be incorporated as required.

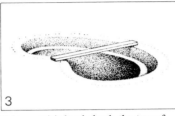

Using a spirit level check the top of
the pool is level. Check that the
depth of the marginal shelf is correct.

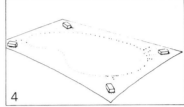

Remove any sharp protrusions and
lay sand on base and dampened
newspaper around sides. Drape
the liner loosely into the excavation with an even overlap. Place
weights on the liner.

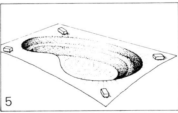

As the pool fills the weights should
be eased off at intervals to allow the
liner to fit snugly into the
excavation.

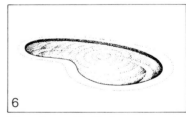

When the pool is filled waste material
should be trimmed off with scissors
leaving a 4 in (10 cm) overlap.

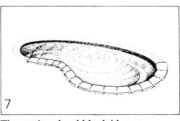

The paving should be laid on a
mortar mix of 3 parts sand/1 part
cement with an overhang of 2 in
(5 cm) over the pool.

The finished pool after planting.
Rockeries, fountains and waterfalls
can be added after completion of
the pool.

14

Installing the Pool Liner

Whatever kind of liner is used, the method of installation is more or less the same, although it is helpful to spread those made from polythene or PVC material out in the sun for an hour or so before working so that they become pliable and mould to the shape of the excavation more easily.

Polythene liners have little elasticity and should be installed without water being added, allowing plenty of room for movement so that when introduced it moulds to the exact contours of the hole. PVC and rubber liners can be stretched across the excavation and weighted down with paving slabs or stones. Water is then added, and as the liner tightens, the anchoring weights on the ground are slowly released until the pool becomes full and the liner moulds exactly to its shape. When the pool is full, and any unsightly wrinkles that might remain have been dealt with, the surplus material around the sides can be trimmed, allowing just sufficient to remain to enable the liner to be secured by paving slabs or rocks. The pool is then ready for immediate planting, for none of the specially designed pool liners contains anything that is likely to prove toxic to aquatic life.

Types of Pre-shaped Pools

Pre-shaped Pools

This quality is also responsible for the increased popularity of pre-shaped pools of plastic or fibreglass for, although the cost of these and concrete ones are comparable, one does not have the tedious task of scrubbing or soaking the surface in order to get rid of the effects of free lime before planting can begin. The cheaper brands of this kind of pool are usually vacuum moulded in a tough, weather-resistant plastic, and have a rough undulating finish to simulate natural rock. Whilst being inexpensive and easily transportable, they do have the disadvantage of flexibility which can cause difficulty during installation, whereas those made from fibreglass are entirely rigid and free-standing.

For the experienced pond owner a fibreglass pool is a splendid investment. It is virtually indestructible, and if treated with respect will last a lifetime. There are dozens of different shapes and sizes, most of which can be obtained in stone, blue, white or a green colour, and I would suggest that the prospective customer sends for several of the excellent illustrated and informative catalogues currently being issued by manufacturers, before making a final choice. Quality and design are the most important features, the latter being particularly important as few pool manufacturers are gardeners and they generally have little idea about the requirements of marginal plants. A hasty purchase, especially at the lower end of the market, will often result in acquiring a pool with slender marginal shelves on which it is impossible to grow anything satisfactorily.

Figure 2.3: An example of a pre-shaped pool with marginal shelves of good proportions

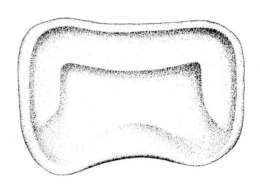

'Rock Pools' or 'Fountain Trays'

When looking through a catalogue be aware of the difference between 'rock pools' or 'fountain trays' and garden pools, for the former are not suitable for plants or fish, although gardeners are attracted to them by their relative cheapness. 'Rock pools' are those designed to sit near the summit of a rock garden and from which water tumbles down a cascade unit into a lower pool. They hold a very small volume of water and cannot sustain any aquatic life, save possibly that of a handful of water snails and a couple of oxygenating plants. 'Fountain trays' are also too shallow; these are the type of pool in which a fountain alone is stood or into which a gargoyle may spout. Owing to the turbulence of water created in this environment little of any significance can be grown, and although ornamental fish would survive they would not be very happy.

Installing a Pre-shaped Pool

Installing a pre-shaped pool is not all that difficult if one knows how to tackle the job properly. Unfortunately, most people attempt to dig out a hole in the shape of the pool — a method doomed to failure. A more practical approach is to dig out a rectangle to enclose the entire outline of the pool. Then place the pool on a thin layer of sand and, by means of bricks and similar materials, level it up so that from side to side and end to end it is completely level and approximately an inch (2$\frac{1}{2}$ cm) below the surface of the surrounding ground. The levelling ensures that when the pool is filled, the water lies evenly and does not drain to one corner and flood the lawn. The idea of the pool being lower than ground level is so that when back-filling takes place the lifting of the pool, which is inevitable when soil is rammed evenly around it, is no more than can be comfortably camouflaged when the job is finished. In soils that are stony or heavy and in poor tilth it is better to back-fill with sand, gradually removing any supporting bricks as the filling replaces them. This should be rammed tightly around the pool, as any air pockets behind it may give rise to subsidence in the future.

Finally, we come to concrete, which if laid properly is still the best form of construction. Not only can it be prepared in several colours, but it can be formed into almost any shape imaginable. The excavation should be taken out 6 in (15 cm) larger than the desired finished size, the soil firmed, and then lined with polythene or building paper before operations commence. It is best if the concreting can be done in one day as there is then less likelihood of a leak occurring. If this proves to be impossible, then the edges of the first day's concreting should be 'roughed up' so that the next day's concrete mixes with it. No more than twenty-four hours should elapse between joining any one batch of concrete and another if the possibility of leaking is to be avoided.

Concrete Construction

Although mixing concrete is hard physical work, there is nothing complicated or mysterious about it. A good mixture consists of one part cement, two parts sand and four parts $\frac{3}{4}$ in (20 mm) gravel measured out with a shovel or bucket. This is then mixed in its dry state until of a uniform greyish colour. If a waterproofing compound is to be added, it should be done at this stage. This usually comes in a powder form and should be mixed in with the aggregate strictly according to the manufacturer's instructions. Water is then added and mixing continued until the agglomeration is of a wet, yet stiff, nature. A good guide to its readiness is to place a shovel into the mixture and withdraw it in a series of jerks; if the ridges thus formed retain their formation, the concrete is ready for laying.

It should be spread evenly to a depth of 4 in (10 cm) over the floor and, if the slope of the sides permits, up these as well. Wire netting can then be placed on the concrete and trapped between the base and final layers to act as reinforcement. The final layer of 2 in (5 cm) is then laid, and given a smooth finish with a plasterer's trowel. If the pool sides are vertical or very steep, formwork may have to be erected. This is usually of rough timber and held in place to form a mould for the walls. To reduce the risk of the concrete sticking to the timbers, they should, strictly speaking, be greased or lime-washed but one can usually get away with soaking the boards in water before pouring the concrete behind them.

Figure 2.4: Pool construction using concrete

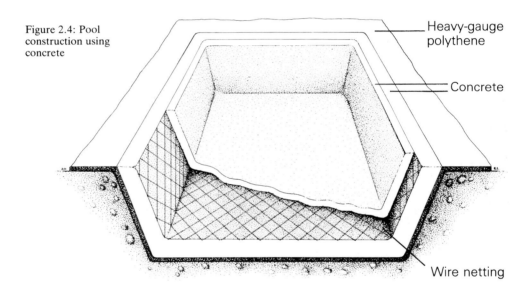

Heavy-gauge polythene

Concrete

Wire netting

When the pool is to be of an irregular shape and the harsh straightness of ordinary planks is undesirable, a successful result can usually be achieved by the careful use of plywood or other pliable material — suitably strengthened with ordinary timbers — and bent to the various contours that are desired.

When a coloured finish is required, the necessary ingredients should be added at the dry-mix stage of the concrete used for the final layer. Pigments mixed in with the cement in any proportion up to 10 per cent by weight of the same, give a good, even colouring. Red iron oxide provides a red colouring, chromium oxide a deep green, cobalt blue a blue, and manganese black a black; whilst the use of Snowcrete cement and fine Derbyshire spar produces a really first-class, white finish.

A couple of hours after completion, when any lingering surface water from the concrete has soaked away, all the exposed areas of concrete should be covered with wet hessian sacks, especially if the weather is warm and sunny. This prevents the concrete from drying too rapidly and hair-cracks appearing. If the area to be covered is large, then regular spraying of the surface with water from a watering can with a fine rose attachment is to be recommended. Depending upon the weather, but after about five days, the concrete should have 'gone off', and be ready for treating prior to the introduction of plants and livestock.

As is well known, concrete contains a substantial amount of free lime, which can be harmful in varying degrees to both plant and fish life. Leaving the pool to the mercy of the elements for about six months is the easiest method of preventing trouble occurring, but few gardeners are prepared to wait this long before introducing some kind of life. Many treatments are recommended by different authorities, and include scrubbing the concrete with potassium permanganate, emptying and refilling the pool upwards of half a dozen times and many other laborious and dubious methods. I would suggest filling the pool with water once and leaving it to stand for a week or ten days and then emptying. When the concrete has dried, an application of a neutralising agent, such as the well-known 'Sylglaze' compound, should completely eliminate the chance of any trouble occurring.

It is also perhaps worth mentioning that in neutralising the lime, a product of this nature reacts to form silica — an insoluble compound — and thus seals the concrete by internal glazing. Rubber-based and liquid plastic paints, when painted over the entire concrete surface, also prevent free lime from escaping but in most cases it must be remembered that a special primer has to be applied first to prevent a chemical reaction between concrete and paint. These paints are available in several pleasing pastel shades and give a splendid finish to the pool, but unfortunately prove rather expensive when there are large areas to be covered.

Before leaving pool construction and turning our attention to the plants we must consider the natural pool. While this requires little in the way of construction, it must be dealt with

Natural Pools

sympathetically from the point of view of planting, for the correct choice and manner of planting is often essential for structural stability. Most gardeners appreciate the scope and pleasure offered by a natural water garden, but the majority are overawed by managing such an asset, while those who have sufficient confidence often mar its aesthetic qualities by trying to formalise its structure or overplant with unsuitable subjects. A natural water garden will only retain its charm if left to develop of its own accord, assisted merely by the addition or exclusion of selected plants and creatures and the occasional removal of excessive mulm from the bottom.

One of the major problems encountered with a natural pool that is totally dependent upon nature is the fluctuating water level. This is serious in so far as it excludes from consideration aquatic plants which will not tolerate such variances, but it should not be allowed to lead to unimaginative planting as there is a wealth of plant life that will live under such conditions and provide suitable growth. These are by and large streamside plants such as reeds and rushes, the common marsh marigold, water mint and water forget-me-not.

Planting is not, of course, just a matter of the harmonious placing of one species alongside another, for depending upon the theme of the feature, subjects may be chosen to fulfil other functions as well as be pleasing to the eye. Obviously in a garden situation high priority will be given to the placement of plants which are in direct line of vision from the dwelling. Taller kinds will be accommodated in the background, leaving the foreground uncluttered and thereby allowing the open water to reflect their beauty.

The subjects chosen for the marginal planting of a natural pool will vary according to soil conditions. Where heavy soil predominates the choice is wide and varied, but when the top soil is light, or overlying gravel, species with creeping rootstocks take precedence in order to bind the soil and prevent erosion. Indeed, erosion is quite a problem, even with small areas of water, for the wind can whip up small waves that can easily damage the banks. Planting through large mesh galvanised wire netting spread along and pegged to the banks is a reliable method of controlling such erosion. The plants eventually grow and completely engulf the netting, hiding it from view, but by intertwining amongst it form a continuous immovable mat the entire perimeter of the pool. Another benefit is that burrowing mammals, which also take their toll on the banks of natural pools, are effectively deterred.

Chapter 3

Hardy Deep Water Aquatics

Gardeners generally regard waterlilies or *Nymphaeas* as the most important decorative plants in the pool, and no wonder, for these gorgeous subjects flower from mid-summer until the first autumn frosts and are available in almost every colour imaginable. Pondlilies or *Nuphars* are useful too, but only where there is constantly running water or shady conditions, for their small bottle-shaped blossoms are rather modest and emit a sickly aroma. Their foliage is waterlily-like and provides a similar visual aspect to that of their more desirable cousins, although in some species it is vigorous and far-spreading and capable of swamping a small pool. The remaining deep water aquatics are complementary to waterlilies providing a contrast of colour, form and foliage, and often extending the flowering season. All require planting and growing in a similar manner. While the methods described here are specific to waterlilies, any additional special requirements of the other species are noted.

Planting Deep Water Aquatics

There are two planting methods commonly advocated for waterlilies and other deep water aquatics. Either the pool floor can be covered with 6 in (15 cm) or so of prepared compost and the plants grown directly in this, or else they can be planted in a container. Most pool owners adopt the latter method as then they have more control over their plants. These can be easily removed for inspection or division, or in the event of the pool needing to be cleaned out. Specially manufactured waterlily baskets are the most suitable and are readily available from most garden centres. Usually they are made of a heavy-gauge, rigid polythene or plastic material and of a design that will not easily become unbalanced and topple over in the water. As they have lattice-work sides, it is advisable to line them with hessian before planting to prevent any compost spillage into the water.

Figure 3.1:
Waterlily planted in
soil covered with a
layer of gravel

The best compost to use for planting waterlilies is good clean garden soil from land that has not recently been dressed with artificial fertiliser. This should be thoroughly sieved, and care taken to remove twigs, pieces of old turf, weeds, old leaves, or indeed anything that is likely to decompose and foul the water. On no account should soil be collected from wet, low-lying land or natural ponds and streams, as this will often contain the seeds of pernicious water weeds which may be difficult to eradicate once they become established in the pool.

The soil having been prepared, a little coarse bonemeal should be added. Allow about a handful for each basket to be planted and mix it thoroughly into the compost. As an alternative a coarse grade of hoof and horn or similar slow-acting nitrogenous fertiliser may also be used, but only sparingly, and not in the popular powdered or granular form, as this will usually cloud the water and may even prove toxic to fish and other livestock. In years gone by cow manure and various other animal manures have been recommended for waterlily culture, and while they unquestionably promote vigorous growth, they also encourage the proliferation of green water-discolouring algae.

Waterlilies and other aquatic plants can be planted successfully in Great Britain and the USA at any time from late April until mid-August. The compost used should be dampened to such a consistency that when squeezed in the hand it binds together, yet is not so wet as to ooze through the fingers.

22

Figure 3.2: Preparing the waterlily for planting — removing dead tissue, etc.

Figure 3.3: Planting the waterlily in a heavy loam compost. The planting basket has first been lined with a square of hessian

Figure 3.4: Filling the basket to within an inch or so of the top. The soil should then be watered to drive out the air

Figure 3.5: Covering the compost with a layer of pea shingle

Before planting take a look at the root-stocks of the waterlilies involved. The rootstocks of *Nymphaea odorata* and *N. tuberosa* and their varieties are long and fleshy, and should be planted horizontally about an inch (2.5 cm) beneath the surface of the compost with just the crown or growing point exposed. The *marliacea* and *laydekeri* hybrids, together with most of the other popular garden varieties and the *Nuphars*, have bulky log-like rootstocks with fibrous roots arranged like a ruff immediately below the crown. These are planted vertically, or at a slight angle, with the crown just protruding above the planting medium.

Figure 3.6:
Nymphaea tuberosa

With both *Nymphaeas* and *Nuphars* it is advisable to remove all the adult leaves at a point just above the crown before planting. This may seem rather drastic, but they would in all probability die anyway, and when planted with the foliage intact this often acts as a float, giving the plant buoyancy and lifting it right out of the basket. The fibrous roots should also be cut back to the rootstock and any dead or decaying area of the rhizome pared back with a knife to live tissue and dressed with powdered charcoal or flowers of sulphur to help seal the wound and prevent infection. If a rootstock takes on a gelatinous appearance and is evil-smelling, avoid making contact with sound varieties, for this is a certain indication of infection with waterlily root-rot.

It is important that when planting, the compost is packed as tightly as possible in the container, for it will be full of air spaces and will decrease in volume considerably as the water drives the air out. Rootstocks of newly planted waterlilies are often left completely exposed following this sinking effect, and where the roots have had insufficient time to penetrate the

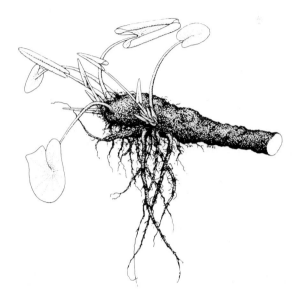

Figure 3.7: Typical hybrid hardy waterlily ready for planting. The 'eye' can be seen quite clearly

compost the whole plant will come floating to the surface. Watering newly planted waterlilies like pot plants prior to placing in their permanent positions usually helps to settle the compost and alleviates this problem. A generous layer of washed pea-shingle an inch (2.5 cm) deep should be spread over the surface of the planting medium to discourage fish from nosing in the compost and clouding the water.

In a newly constructed pool the planted baskets should be placed in their required positions and enough water run in to cover the crowns. As the young foliage appears the water level can be gradually raised. It is inadvisable to plunge freshly planted waterlilies directly into 2 or 3 ft (60-90 cm) of cold water unless absolutely necessary, for they have already suffered a considerable shock by being moved and defoliated whilst in active growth without having to fight their way to the surface of the water. When merely adding a plant to an established pool, then this procedure can be reversed, the basket being stood on a pile of bricks and gradually lowered by removing the bricks one by one as the growths lengthen. When baskets have to be placed in an awkward position in the centre of the pool, lengths of string can be threaded through either side of the basket, and with one person each side of the pool can be carefully lowered into place.

When planting into compost on the pool floor all the same general rules apply as far as is practicable. It follows though, that if a hosepipe is placed directly into the pool and turned on, the stream of water will stir up the soil and the pool will become cloudy. By placing the end of the hosepipe on a large sheet of polythene and allowing the water to trickle over the edge this is prevented. As the water level rises the polythene is lifted and trapped against the end of the hosepipe, which, if the sheet is large enough, will also be gradually raised until the water is at the desired level.

Gardeners who are in the fortunate position of having a natural pond will have to adopt a different planting technique which in many ways conflicts with the advice just proffered. However, one cannot fight nature, and as most of the waterlilies and other deep water aquatics used in the planting of natural ponds are fairly vigorous, the somewhat unconventional methods outlined usually work satisfactorily. The major problem is that natural pools are not easily emptied and so planting has to take place through the water. The best method is to plant in the same compost as described earlier on squares of hessian. The four corners of the hessian are then lifted and tied just beneath the crown. These 'packages' can then be gently placed in the water and allowed to sink to the bottom. The hessian will eventually rot, but by that time the plants will be well established in the compost and will probably have penetrated the surrounding mud on the pool floor.

The positioning of waterlilies in the pool should be carefully considered if they are to give of their best. Due regard must be paid to the depth of water available, which in turn will determine, within limits, the varieties which can be successfully grown. Moving water restricts the number of plants which can be safely accommodated for few waterlilies will tolerate even the slightest movement of the water, and therefore *Nuphars* or other deep water aquatics will have to be considered in pools where a fountain is constantly playing. Sunlight is also important, plants being placed in positions where they can receive the maximum amount, and where this is difficult to arrange and an area is shaded for much of the time, then of the deep water subjects, only the *Nuphars* are likely to flourish.

Hardy Deep Water Aquatics

Waterlilies and other deep water aquatics are not difficult to maintain once established. All that is required is vigilance in observing any pests and diseases that may arise, and ensuring that the plants are well fed and divided every third or fourth year as necessary. Difficulty is often experienced in feeding the plants without having to resort to lifting and dividing them. Modern waterlily fertilisers are now produced in perforated sachets that are merely pushed into the compost in the containers adjacent to the plants. These sachets are very good, but rather expensive when there is a sizeable collection of plants to treat. A simple alternative is to make bonemeal 'pills' which are pushed into the compost alongside the plants. These are made with a handful of coarse bonemeal and sufficient wet clay soil to bind it together and merely rolled into a sticky ball. Whether modern fertilisers are used or the bonemeal method adopted, it is important to ensure that all aquatic plants receive periodic feeding. Deficiency is usually quite marked, particularly with waterlilies which get progressively smaller, sport yellowing foliage and blooms of poor colour with few petals. This can also be indicative of over-crowding, particularly when the plant produces foliage that seems to climb out of the water on the backs of its neighbours and blossoming is much depressed. With most varieties this condition manifests itself after three or four years, although some of the smaller growing varieties may go for as long as six or seven years without needing attention.

Feeding Deep Water Aquatics

May is the best time to divide waterlilies in Great Britain, each plant being lifted and washed, and any adult foliage removed at source.

Dividing Waterlilies

It will be seen that each plant consists of a main rootstock from which several 'eyes' have grown to form sizeable 'branches', and it is these side growths that should be retained, cutting them from the parent plant with as much rootstock as possible. The thick bulky part of the original plant is generally of little use and should be discarded, but all the 'branches' can be planted individually to form new plants, providing that they each have a healthy terminal shoot.

Of course waterlilies, and to a lesser degree pondlilies, can be lifted deliberately during late April or early May in order to propagate them. Most varieties produce 'eyes' which provide a ready means of increasing one's stock. As mentioned above,

Propagating Waterlilies

27

'eyes' are tiny growing points which occur with varying frequency along the rootstocks of mature hardy waterlilies. In most cases they appear as smaller versions of the main growing point, each with its own juvenile foliage seeming ready to burst into active growth, although in *Nymphaea tuberosa* and its varieties they take the form of brittle rounded nodules which are easily detached.

The pool owner who wishes to increase his waterlilies should remove the 'eyes' with a sharp knife. The wounds of both 'eye' and rootstock must then be dusted with powdered charcoal or flowers of sulphur to prevent infection and the parent plant can be returned to the pool. Individual 'eyes' are then potted into small pots in a good stiff, loam compost and stood in a shallow container to which has been added sufficient water to cover the rims of the pots. If the 'eyes' are very small it is advisable to give them the added protection of a cold frame or greenhouse during the initial stages of growth. As they develop the water level must be raised and the plants potted into successively larger pots until a 4 in (10 cm) size is attained, after which it can be safely assumed that they will be capable of holding their own in the outdoor pool. As waterlilies resent the close confines of a pot, better results can be obtained by potting the young plants into lattice-work plant pot covers which are used quite frequently in homes to disguise the red-brown of the pots in which house plants are commonly grown.

Growing Waterlilies from Seed

At the outset, few pool owners will feel the need or indeed be competent to grow waterlilies from seed. However, the process by which they are grown applies in broad terms to many other aquatics and is consequently worth relating here. If one is dealing with waterlilies, then the opportunities for producing the hardy kinds from seed is very limited for only *N. tetragona* and *N. pygmaea* 'Alba' produce seed regularly, or in fact come uniform and true to type from seed.

It is seldom possible to acquire seed other than directly from a fruiting plant and as *Nymphaea* seed is very vulnerable to drying out, this is the best method of obtaining it. The seeds of both *N. tetragona* and *N. pygmaea* 'Alba' form greenish-white fruits which become submerged immediately the flowers fade. They reappear at the surface again some three weeks later, and if not collected immediately will burst open and scatter their contents in the water. The pods should be gathered after they have been submerged for about ten days, detached with as much old flower stem as possible, and placed in a shallow dish of water so that when they ripen the seed will not be lost. Alternatively, a small muslin bag can be used to enclose the seed pod and removed from the plant immediately the pod bursts. When the fruits are ripe they will be clearly seen to exude a clear gelatinous substance in which the seeds are embodied. This sticky jelly should be sown with the seeds.

Finely sieved garden soil of the kind recommended for the planting of waterlilies is the best sowing medium and this should be put in shallow seed pans. The seeds are then sown, the jelly-like carrier being spread over the surface of the compost with a pair of tweezers. A light covering of soil can then be given and the pans sprayed gently overhead from a watering can in order to settle the compost. They can then be stood in a deep bowl or aquarium with the water just lapping over the surface of the compost, and placed in a warm sunny position.

After three weeks or so the first seedlings will appear. They have tiny, translucent, roughly lanceolate leaves, and look very much like an aquatic liverwort. During this time, and indeed for the first six months of their life, filamentous algae is likely to cause problems by becoming entangled amongst the fragile juvenile foliage of the seedlings. This can be controlled by the prompt use of an algaecide, but it is essential to remove the destroyed remains of the algae or else fermentation will occur with the subsequent rotting of the waterlily foliage. When the first two or three small floating leaves have come to the surface the plants can be pricked out. They should be lifted in clumps, washed thoroughly to remove all the soil, and then gently teased apart. A standard plastic seed tray or plastic half pots are the most useful containers in which to prick out the seedlings, which should then be immersed so that the compost is about an inch (2.5 cm) beneath the surface of the water. This level can be raised considerably as the growths lengthen and become much stronger. After six months the plants will begin to crowd one another, when they should be lifted and moved to their permanent quarters.

The figures in parenthesis refer to the depths at which each individual plant is most successfully grown.

Popular Waterlily Species and Their Varieties

Nymphaea alba Common White Waterlily. This is a handsome waterlily for the larger pool, where once established it will produce a succession of glistening white blossoms amongst handsome orbicular fresh green foliage. Not suitable for the average garden pool, but often sold by pet shops and garden centres as 'white waterlilies' at a very low price. Should be avoided unless you have plenty of room and a good depth of water. (up to 10 ft (3 m))

N. candida An excellent hardy species for shallow water. It produces an abundance of small white cup-shaped blossoms with golden stamens and crimson stigmas. Many forms of this species have been described, but are rarely encountered in cultivation. (1-1$\frac{1}{2}$ ft (30-45 cm))

N. caroliniana A lovely fragrant soft pink variety with slender petals and conspicuous yellow stamens. The leaves are pale green. Three cultivars derived from *N. caroliniana* are often encountered: the pure white 'Nivea', rose-pink 'Rosea' and salmon-pink 'Perfecta'. (1-1$\frac{1}{2}$ ft (30-45 cm))

N. odorata Sweet Scented Waterlily. This is an excellent species for the small or medium-sized pool. Fragrant white flowers up to 6 in (15 cm) in diameter float on the surface of the water amongst handsome pea-green leaves. All the natural variants and hybrids derived from *N. odorata* have distinctive circular leaves that make them easily separated from any other species. *Nymphaea odorata* var. *rosea*, the Cape Cod Waterlily, is the most popular variety having deep pink blossoms with bright yellow stamens, but for the tiny pool *N. odorata* var. *minor*, the Mill Pond Waterlily, is hard to surpass with its starry white flowers and rich heady fragrance.

Hybrids Derived Directly From *Nymphaea odorata*

'Eugene de Land' This bears exquisite star-shaped blossoms of deep glowing apricot-pink which are held well above the water. The petals are somewhat incurved and the stamens are a deep golden-yellow. It is richly fragrant. (1$\frac{1}{2}$-2$\frac{1}{2}$ ft (45-75 cm))

'Firecrest' This waterlily has striking purplish leaves and deep pink flowers with curious red-tipped stamens. (1$\frac{1}{2}$-3 ft (45-90 cm))

'Sulphurea' The canary-yellow flowers of this waterlily are star-shaped, fragrant, and consist of numerous slender petals. It has very distinctive dark green, heavily mottled foliage. (1 ft (30 cm))

'Sulphurea Grandiflora' This is an improved form of the preceding and larger in every respect. (1$\frac{1}{2}$-2 ft (45-60 cm))

Figure 3.8:
Nymphaea
'Firecrest'

'Turicensis' This bears very fragrant soft rose-pink blooms not
unlike those of *N. odorata* var. *rosea*. (1^{1}2-2^{1}2 ft (45-75 cm))
'William B. Shaw' This is probably the most desirable of the
odorata types. Its large open creamy-pink flowers have deep
red internal zoning and are held well clear of the fresh green
foliage. (1^{1}2-2 ft (45-60 cm))

N. tetragona Pygmy White Waterlily. This is a tiny white-
flowered species with small dark green leaves with purplish
undersides. The blossoms are seldom more than 1 in (2.5
cm) across, are fragrant, and have bright golden stamens.
Many geographical forms are known to botanists, but these
seldom find their way into cultivation. The pink-flowered
mutant, 'Johann Pring' is more frequently available and can
be highly recommended for sink or rock pool. (6 in-1 ft (15-
30 cm))

N. tuberosa Magnolia Waterlily. This strong-growing, almost
scentless species has pure white cup-shaped flowers 4 to 6 in
(10 to 15 cm) across. The large orbicular leaves are bright
green. The pink flowered *N. tuberosa* var. *rosea* and cool
icy-white 'Richardsonii' are the best forms for the garden
pool, although they require plenty of space to develop. (2-4
ft (60 cm-1 m 20 cm))

Waterlily
Hybrids

All the following hybrids are of unknown or partially discernible origin and are arranged alphabetically. Three distinctive groups, the *laydekeri* and *marliacea* hybrids, and the *pygmaea* varieties are gathered together as they all have similar characteristics.

'Alaska' This recent introduction has flowers up to 6 in (15 cm) across, extremely wide petals and a dense boss of long yellow stamens. Has proved to be very hardy. (2-3 ft (60-90 cm))

'Albatross' A medium growing variety with large pure-white blooms surrounding a central cluster of golden stamens. The leaves are purplish when young but change to deep green when fully expanded. (1-2 ft (30-60 cm))

'Amabilis' (syn. 'Pink Marvel') Large stellate salmon-pink flowers up to 10 in (25 cm) across which deepen to soft rose with age. The bright yellow stamens also intensify to a fiery orange. The leaves are large and deep green. (1½-2 ft (45-60 cm))

'Andreana' The deep brick-red cup-shaped blossoms are up to 8 in (20 cm) across, and streaked and shaded with cream and yellow. They are supported on stout stems 3 or 4 in (7 or 10 cm) above the water. The bold, glossy-green foliage is blotched with maroon and characterised by overlapping lobes. (2-3 ft (60-90 cm))

'Arethusa' Large rounded deep rose-pink flowers intensifying to crimson towards the centre. The rose-pink outer petals are tipped with light red. (1½-2 ft (45-60 cm))

'Attraction' The large garnet-red flowers of this variety are attractively flecked with white and may be 9 in (23 cm) or so across when fully expanded. Its rich mahogany stamens are tipped with yellow and the sepals are off-white infused with rose-pink. The foliage is large and green. (2-4 ft (60 cm-1 m 20 cm))

'Aurora' This delightful little plant has purplish mottled leaves and flowers that change colour day by day. The buds are cream, opening to yellow, and finally pass through orange to blood-red. (1-1½ ft (30-45 cm))

'Baroness Orczy' This variety has large deep rose-pink, cup-shaped blooms and is excellent for the medium-sized pool. (1½-2 ft (45-60 cm))

'Charles de Meurville' A strong-growing variety with large plum-coloured blossoms tipped and streaked with white, but which age to deep wine amongst handsome olive-green foliage. (2-4 ft (60 cm-1 m 20 cm))

'Comanche' The small deep orange blooms which change to bronze with age, are held well clear of the surface of the water. The leaves are purplish when young, but rapidly turn green as they unfurl. (1-$1\frac{1}{2}$ ft (30-45 cm))

'Conqueror' The large crimson cup-shaped flowers are flecked with white. They have broad incurving petals, bright yellow stamens and conspicuous sepals with white interiors. The young foliage is purple, but eventually changes to green. ($1\frac{1}{2}$-2 ft (45-60 cm))

'Ellisiana' The small wine-red flowers with orange stamens are produced in abundance. It is one of the easiest and most reliable hardy waterlily hybrids. (1-2 ft (30-60 cm))

'Escarboucle' (syn. 'Aflame') The large crimson flowers up to 1 ft (30 cm) across have central clusters of golden-yellow stamens and are richly fragrant. A truly magnificent plant, but requires plenty of room to do it justice. (2-6 ft (60 cm-1 m 80 cm))

'Fabiola' The warm rosy-red blossoms are flushed with white and sport conspicuous nut-brown stamens. The foliage is deep green. ($1\frac{1}{2}$-2 ft (45-60 cm))

Figure 3.9:
Nymphaea
'Froebeli'

'Froebeli' This waterlily has deep blood-red flowers with orange stamens and dull, purplish-green leaves. It is one of the most popular and free-flowering varieties for the garden pool and has a delicious fragrance. ($1\frac{1}{2}$-2 ft (45-60 cm))

'Galatee' The white flowers are heavily overlaid with red, producing an extraordinary piebald effect. The dark green leaves are splashed with maroon. ($1\frac{1}{2}$-3 ft (45-90 cm))

'Gladstoniana' The exceptionally large pure white flowers are like huge floating soup dishes. The broad curved petals of a thick waxy texture surround a cluster of golden thread-like stamens. The large dark green lily pads have stalks that are distinctly marked with brown. A beautiful variety, but can only be seen to advantage in a large expanse of water, although often offered by garden centres as suitable for the garden pool. (2-8 ft (60 cm-2 m 40 cm))

'Gloire de Temple sur Lot' A really choice variety that can take a couple of years to become established and flower freely. The fragrant fully double flowers have rosy-pink incurving petals — a hundred or more to each bloom — and change to pure white with age. The stamens are bright yellow. ($1\frac{1}{2}$-3 ft (45-90 cm))

'Gloriosa' (syn. 'Glory') The very fragrant flowers of deep currant-red float on the surface of the water. Each blossom is 6 in (15 cm) or more across with five conspicuous sepals and a cluster of bright reddish-orange stamens. The leaves are orbicular and dull bronze-green. ($1\frac{1}{2}$-3 ft (45-90 cm))

'Gonnere' (syn. 'Crystal White') The pure white, double, globular flowers have conspicuous green sepals. The luxuriant pea-green leaves have a very modest spread, making this an excellent plant for the medium-sized pool. ($1\frac{1}{2}$-$2\frac{1}{2}$ ft (45-75 cm))

'Graziella' The orange-red flowers are scarcely 2 in (5 cm) across, have deep orange stamens and are produced in abundance throughout the summer. The olive-green leaves are blotched with brown and purple. This is an ideal waterlily for sink or tub culture. (1-2 ft (30-60 cm))

'Hermine' (syn. 'Hermione') The tulip-shaped blooms of purest white are held slightly above its distinctive dark green oval foliage. ($1\frac{1}{2}$-$2\frac{1}{2}$ ft (45-75 cm))

'Indiana' The orange-red flowers age to deep red and rest amongst foliage that is heavily blotched and splashed with purple. ($1\frac{1}{2}$-$2\frac{1}{2}$ ft (45-75 cm))

'James Brydon' The large, fragrant, crimson paeony-shaped flowers float amidst dark purplish-green leaves that are flecked with maroon. The stamens are deep orange tipped with bright yellow. ($1\frac{1}{2}$-3 ft (45-90 cm))

A group of hybrids suitable for the smaller pool which were raised by the famous waterlily hybridist Marliac and named after his son-in-law Maurice Laydeker. All grow best in 1-2 ft (30-60 cm) of water.

laydekeri 'Alba' The snow-white blossoms with yellow stamens give off a strong aroma reminiscent of a freshly opened packet of tea

laydekeri 'Fulgens' The fragrant, bright crimson flowers have reddish stamens and dark green sepals with rose-blush interiors. The leaves are dark green with purplish undersides and brown speckling in the region of the petiole

laydekeri 'Lilacea' The soft pink fragrant flowers age to a deep rosy-crimson. The stamens are bright yellow and the sepals dark green edged with rose. The glossy green leaves are sparsely blotched with brown

laydekeri 'Purpurata' This is one of the most outstanding hardy varieties currently available. The rich vinous-red flowers are produced from late April until the first autumn frosts, and during the height of the season there may be upwards of two dozen blooms on a well established plant at any one time. The individual blossoms are composed of numerous acutely pointed petals and a striking bunch of bright orange stamens. The leaves are comparatively small, purple beneath, and often marked on the surface with black or maroon splashes

'Louise' This recently introduced cultivar has deep red, fully double, cup-shaped blossoms with petals that are tipped with white. The stamens are yellow and the sepals brownish-green. (2-3 ft (60-90 cm))

A group of vigorous waterlilies raised by Marliac and given his name. They are all of indeterminate origin, but contain some of the best and easiest varieties the gardener can grow.

marliacea 'Albida' (syn. 'Marliac White') The large, pure white, fragrant blooms are held just above the water. The sepals and backs of the petals are often flushed with soft pink, and the large deep green leaves have red or purplish undersides. (1½-3 ft (45-90 cm))

marliacea 'Carnea' (syns. 'Marliac Flesh', 'Mary Exquisita', 'Morning Glory') This very strong growing flesh-pink hybrid has stellate blossoms 8 or more in (20 cm) across with golden stamens. The flowers on newly established plants are often white for the first few months. It is an excellent cut-flower variety with a strong vanilla fragrance. The leaves are large, purplish when young, but turn deep green when mature. (1½-5 ft (45 cm-1 m 50 cm))

marliacea 'Chromatella' (syns. 'Marliac Yellow', 'Golden Cup') This is an old and very popular variety with 6 in (15 cm) wide blossoms of rich canary-yellow. The petals are broad and incurved with deep golden stamens and the pale yellow sepals are flushed with pink. It is slightly fragrant and produces olive-green leaves which are boldly splashed with maroon and bronze. (1½-2½ ft (45-75 cm))

Figure 3.10:
*Nymphaea
marliacea*
'Chromatella'

marliacea 'Flammea' The fiery red flowers are flecked with white, the outer petals are deep pink and the stamens rich orange. The olive-green leaves are heavily mottled with chocolate and maroon. (1½-2½ ft (45-75 cm))

marliacea 'Rosea' (syns. 'Marliac Pink', 'Marliac Rose') Differs from *marliacea* 'Carnea' in the intensity of colouring, its petals being infused with a deep rosy flush. It is very fragrant. The foliage is purplish-green when young and dark green when mature. (1½-4 ft (45 cm-1 m 20 cm))

'Masaniello' The fragrant rose-pink, cup-shaped flowers, liberally sprinkled with flecks of crimson and ageing to deep carmine, are held just above the water. The stamens are intense orange and the sepals white. (1½-3 ft (45-90 cm))

'Meteor' The crimson flowers are streaked with white which disappears with age. The stamens are bright yellow and the sepals striped with red. The deep green leaves have purplish undersides. (1½-2½ ft (45-75 cm))

36

'Moorei' (syn. 'Mooreana') A very fine soft yellow variety with distinctive pale green foliage irregularly sprinkled with purple spots. ($1\frac{1}{2}$-$2\frac{1}{2}$ ft (45-75 cm))

'Mrs Richmond' The beautiful pale rose-pink flowers pass to crimson with age. The bases of the petals are bright red and the stamens a rich golden yellow. The sepals are tipped with white. ($1\frac{1}{2}$-$2\frac{1}{2}$ ft (45-75 cm))

'Newton' The deep rosy-peach flowers with white sepals are held above the water. The extra long pointed petals give the blossoms a star-like appearance. The stamens are bright orange. ($1\frac{1}{2}$-$2\frac{1}{2}$ ft (45-75 cm))

'Pearl of the Pool' The clear fully double, bright pink blossoms look as if they are made of icing sugar. The stamens are yellow and the orbicular foliage plain green, coppery beneath. ($1\frac{1}{2}$-$2\frac{1}{2}$ ft (45-75 cm))

'Pink Sensation' This is an extremely fragrant free-flowering pink variety with star-like blossoms which remain open well into the evening. The individual blooms may be up to 8 in (20 cm) across and have distinctive oval petals some 4 in (10 cm) long. The rounded deep green leaves have reddish undersides. ($1\frac{1}{2}$-$2\frac{1}{2}$ ft (45-75 cm))

Pygmaea Hybrids

The pygmy waterlilies are excellent for sinks, troughs or pools where the water does not exceed a foot (30 cm) in depth, or on the marginal shelves of larger pools.

pygmaea 'Alba' The tiniest white waterlily. Each blossom is scarcely an inch (2.5 cm) across and is identical to its larger cousins in all respects. The small oval dark green leaves have purple reverses.

Figure 3.11:
Pygmaea 'Helvola'

pygmaea 'Helvola' (syn. 'Pygmy Yellow') The beautiful canary-yellow flowers with orange stamens are produced continuously throughout the summer. The olive-green foliage is heavily mottled with purple and brown.

pygmaea 'Rubra' The tiny blood-red flowers with orange stamens float amidst purplish-green leaves that have distinctive reddish undersides.

'Rene Gerard' The broad open flowers with narrow rose-pink petals are blotched and splashed with crimson towards the centre. The foliage is plain green. ($1\frac{1}{2}$-$2\frac{1}{2}$ ft (45-75 cm))

'Rose Arey' This is one of the best loved rose-pink varieties. The large, open stellate flowers have a central boss of golden stamens and an overpowering aniseed fragrance. The fine green leaves are tinged with red and the juvenile foliage is crimson. ($1\frac{1}{2}$-$2\frac{1}{2}$ ft (45-75 cm))

'Sioux' Almost identical to N. 'Aurora', the pale yellow blooms pass through orange to crimson, the individual petals being acutely pointed and delicately spotted with red. The dark olive-green foliage has a purplish mottling. (1-$1\frac{1}{2}$ ft (30-45 cm))

'Somptuosa' This early-flowering waterlily produces large fragrant double pink blooms. The stamens are vivid orange and contrast markedly with the soft velvety petals. ($1\frac{1}{2}$-2 ft (45-60 cm))

'Sunrise' The large fragrant, soft canary-yellow blooms are up to 8 in (20 cm) across. The dull green elliptical leaves are occasionally blotched with brown and have reddish undersides and undulating margins. The undersides of both the leaves and petioles are pubescent. ($1\frac{1}{2}$-3 ft (45-90 cm))

'Virginalis' This is a real gem for the medium-sized pool. It bears wonderful semi-double flowers of the purest white. The sepals are rose tinged towards their bases and the stamens are bright yellow. The foliage is green flushed with purple. ($1\frac{1}{2}$-$2\frac{1}{2}$ ft (45-75 cm))

Pondlilies or Spatterdocks

Nuphar advena American Spatterdock. A variable species for sun or shade. It has large, thick, fresh green leaves which float on the surface of the water and clusters of upright foliage which stands erect from the vigorous crown. The globular yellow flowers are about 3 in (8 cm) across, are tinged with purple or green, and have bright coppery-red stamens. ($1\frac{1}{2}$-5 ft (45 cm-1 m 50 cm))

N. japonica Japanese Pondlily. This has large slender, arrow-shaped floating leaves and curled, translucent underwater foliage. The small yellow flowers are up to 3 in (8 cm) across. It only prospers in still water. ($1^{1}2$-$2^{1}2$ ft (45-75 cm))

N. lutea Yellow Pondlily, Brandy Bottle. The bottle-shaped yellow flowers emit a sickly alcoholic odour and are produced amongst masses of leathery, green, ovate floating leaves. (1-8 ft (30 cm-2 m 40 cm))

Figure 3.12: *Nuphar lutea* — Yellow Pondlily, Brandy Bottle

N. minimum Dwarf Pondlily, Least Yellow Pondlily. There is tremendous confusion amongst botanists as to whether this is the same plant as that referred to as *N. pumilum*. To the gardener this is of little account as both, if indeed they are different, are very much alike in appearance. They have small, almost heart-shaped leaves and tiny yellow blossoms. (1-$1^{1}2$ ft (30-45 cm))

N. rubrodisca Red Disked Pond Lily. The large yellow flowers have bright crimson central stigmatic discs. The handsome crinkled submerged foliage is long, floating or occasionally erect. (1-3 ft (30-90 cm))

Other Deep Water Aquatics

Aponogeton distachyus Water Hawthorn. This is a most reliable pond plant, being almost evergreen, and providing a continuous display of blossoms from April until early November in favourable years. The white flowers are forked and bear a double row of bract-like organs at the base of which are clusters of jet-black stamens. A deliciously fragrant plant that bears its floating blossoms amongst dull

Figure 3.13:
*Aponogeton
distachyus* — Water
Hawthorn

green, more or less oblong leaves, which are often heavily
splashed and spotted with purple. (1-3 ft (30-90 cm))

Nymphoides peltata (syn. *Villarsia nymphoides*) Water Fringe.
This lovely little aquatic provides a wonderful display of
delicately fringed buttercup-like flowers during late summer
amongst handsome green and brown mottled foliage, very
much like that of a pygmy waterlily and for this reason it is
often referred to as 'the poor man's waterlily.' Although
Nymphoides can be raised from seed, they are more usually
increased from divisions of the scrambling rootstock (1-2½
ft (30-75 cm))

Orontium aquaticum Golden Club. This is one of the most
bizarre and adaptable aquatic plants one can introduce to
the garden pool. It will grow equally well in wet mud or up
to 18 in (45 cm) of water and provide a striking display of
yellow and white pencil-like flowers during April and early
May. These stand out of the water above waxy glaucous
floating foliage, and yield small greenish fruits which, if
allowed to ripen, provide seed which germinates freely when
sown fresh.

CHAPTER 4

Marginal Plants

The marginal plants are those that grow in the shallows around the edge of the pool, living happily in wet soil or as much as 6 in (15 cm) of water. In the garden pool marginal subjects are usually accommodated on specially constructed shelves, either in properly designed aquatic plant baskets, or directly into soil spread along their length. This latter method cannot be generally recommended, for the invasive species rapidly swamp their more restrained neighbours and spoil the overall visual effect. The compost used for marginal plants is the same as that advocated for waterlilies and other deep water aquatics, and cultural treatment follows along broadly similar lines.

Planting
Marginal
Plants

Figure 4.1: Preparing marginal plants for planting by separating out each plant. The basket has been prepared as for deep water aquatic plants (see pp. 21-2)

Figure 4.2: Planting marginal plants in a basket

Figure 4.3: A generous layer of pea gravel to prevent fish stirring up the compost

Marginal
Plants

Acorus calamus Sweet Flag. This member of the Arum family is often taken to be an iris on account of its clumps of flat linear leaves and fat fleshy rhizomes. The shiny fresh green foliage has a strong tangerine fragrance and supports curious greenish-yellow horn-like flower spikes. The cultivar 'Variegatus' is most desirable, sporting handsome cream, green and rose striped foliage of more modest habit.

A. gramineus This is a dwarf grassy species and like the common sweet flag has an attractive variegated foliage form, 'Variegatus'.

Alisma plantago-aquatica Water Plantain. This is a handsome native with attractive ovate foliage and loose pyramidal panicles of pink and white flowers. The towering spires become hard and woody after flowering and are excellent for cutting for winter decoration indoors.

A. parviflora Of similar habit to our native water plantain, this North American cousin has distinctive rounded leaves and somewhat shorter pyramids of pink and white flowers.

A. ranunculoides More correctly known now as *Baldellia ranunculoides*. This little fellow has delicate arching stems which bend down and root wherever they touch moist soil, rapidly forming a dense spreading colony of bright green lanceolate foliage, studded throughout late summer and early autumn with crowded umbels of rose and blush flowers.

Butomus umbellatus Flowering Bush. A handsome rush-like aquatic which produces spreading umbels of dainty rose-pink flowers during August and September. It reproduces freely from the small bulbils which appear where the leaves join the rhizome. If these are gathered and pushed into a

Figure 4.4: *Butomus umbellatus* — Flowering Bush, and *Scirpus tabernaemontani* 'Zebrinus' — Zebra rush

pot of heavy compost and then grown on in a bowl or tank with an inch (2.5 cm) of water covering them, they quickly form young plants.

Calla palustris Bog Arum. This is a most useful plant for disguising the edge of the pool, for it spreads in all directions by means of stout creeping rhizomes which are clothed in handsome, glossy, heart-shaped foliage. The small icy-white flowers are like miniature versions of the florists' arum, but not so beautifully formed. These are followed by spikes of succulent red berries which contain viable seed that germinates freely if sown immediately. The winter buds which form along the trailing rhizomes can be removed before they start into active growth in the spring. If placed in trays of mud, these too will quickly form healthy young plants.

Caltha palustris Marsh Marigold. Most people are familiar with this lovely native swamp plant which during spring is garlanded with waxy blossoms of intense golden-yellow. It has a marvellous fully double form with bright yellow blossoms, like those of a pompom dahlia, on a compact plant with handsome dark green glossy foliage. The white marsh marigold, *C. palustris alba*, is not so spectacular, producing off-white flowers and foliage that is very prone to mildew. In my estimation the mountain marigold, *C. leptosepala*, is a much better proposition for the gardener who requires a white marsh marigold. This is larger in every respect than the white form of *C. palustris*, but has beautifully sculptured blossoms with a silvery tinge.

C. polypetala Himalayan Marsh Marigold. A giant of a plant in all respects, not infrequently attaining a height of 3 feet (90 cm) or more. Its dark green leaves can be as much as 10 in (25 cm) across and provide a perfect foil for the huge trusses of golden flowers.

Figure 4.5: *Caltha polypetala* — Himalayan Marsh Marigold

All the marsh marigolds are extremely tolerant of situation, flourishing in either wet soil or up to 1 ft (30 cm) of water, but being more compact and attractive under shallower conditions. Propagation of the double form is by division and also more convenient for the species, although these germinate freely from freshly gathered seed.

Carex pendula Pendulous Sedge. One of the few sedges that can be unreservedly recommended for the garden pool. A tall dignified plant with broad green leaves and long drooping spikes of khaki catkin-like flowers that look marvellous when reflected in the water at the poolside. Although a marginal subject, this species prefers moist soil and gives of its best when advancing from the garden into the pool.

C. riparia Great Pond Sedge. This species in its natural form should be avoided by the small pool owner as it is very invasive. However, it has yielded two coloured foliage varieties that are most desirable acquisitions. The strikingly variegated *C. riparia* 'Variegata' is the most reliable, performing well in just damp soil or several inches of water. The golden leafed 'Aurea' is not so persistent, but is well worth trying, its rich golden foliage with contrasting spikes of dark brown flowers illuminating the poolside during early summer. While *C. pendula* and *C. riparia* are readily increased by seed, the foliage forms are only reliable from divisions made during early spring.

Cyperus longus Umbrella Grass, Sweet Galingale. This is a handsome grassy plant which is closely related to the popular indoor house plant *Cyperus alternifolius*, the umbrella plant. Attaining a height of 3 ft (90 cm), or occasionally more, this slender plant has fresh green grassy foliage and terminal umbels of stiff, spiky leaves which radiate from the stem like the ribs of an umbrella. Adaptable to most pool conditions, but at its happiest when growing on a bank and allowed to creep down and colonise the mud at the water's edge.

C. vegetus (syn. *C. eragrostis*) This species is even more akin to the indoor umbrella plant than *C. longus*. It is more compact, very hardy, and produces tufted spikelets of reddish-mahogany flowers throughout late summer from amidst spreading umbels of bright green foliage. Both species grow readily from seed or division of the creeping rootstocks.

Damasonium alisma (syn. *D. stellatum*) Starfruit, Thrum-wort. A rare native that many gardeners would perhaps not consider worthy of inclusion in a small pool. It is a plant for which I have a strong affection though, producing stout upright spikes of milky-white blooms followed by curious star-shaped fruits full of viable seed. The leaves are strap-shaped and arise from a hard corm-like rootstock which in large plants can be divided.

Eriophorum angustifolium (syn. *E. polystachyon*) Cotton Grass. All the cotton grass species are useful for the small pool owner, although they must have acid growing conditions. This is the commonest species and has evergreen grassy foliage sprinkled during May and early June with cotton wool-like seeding heads which if picked in their full glory can be dried for floral decoration.

E. latifolium Broad Leafed Cotton Grass. Not so easy to grow as *E. angustifolium*, but very lovely once established. Broad grass-like foliage smothered in cotton wool-like heads. Both this and the preceding are easily increased by division in the spring.

Glyceria aquatica 'Variegata' Variegated Water Grass. A handsome perennial grass with cream and green striped foliage which on emerging in early spring is infused with deep rose pink. Can be readily propagated by division in the early spring.

Houttuynia cordata (syn. *H. foetida*) A most amenable subject for the small or medium-sized pool with bluish-green heart-shaped leaves and white four-petalled flowers with hard central cones which, in the beautiful double form 'Plena', are lost in a dense central ruff of petals. A splendid plant for carpeting the ground between taller growing rushes and easily increased by division.

Hypericum elodes Marsh Hypericum. This tiny relative of the Rose of Sharon is an extremely useful plant for shallow water or wet mud. It forms a dense carpet of foliage that is ideal for masking that difficult area where pool meets garden, and produces sparkling yellow blossoms during summer. It can be increased by division, or short cuttings taken during the growing season which can be rooted in a pot or tray of mud.

Iris laevigata This is the lovely blue iris of the Asian paddy fields and has given rise to innumerable attractive hybrids. There is the lovely violet and white 'Colchesteri', snowy-white 'Alba' and delicate pink 'Rose Queen'. A lot of confusion exists between *I. laevigata* and its hybrids and those of the Clematis-flowered Iris of Japan *I. kaempferi*. Both groups attain a height of perhaps 2½ ft (75 cm), blossom during June and July, and come from the same part of the world. *I. kaempferi*, and its progeny, however, are not true aquatics, tolerating standing water during the summer months, but fading away if obliged to do so throughout the winter. While superficially alike, the observant gardener will notice that the leaves of *I. laevigata* and its progeny are smooth, whereas those of *I. kaempferi* have a prominent mid-rib. The mention of foliage calls to mind *I. laevigata* 'Variegata' in which all the sword-like leaves are boldly striped with cream.

I. pseudacorus Yellow Flag. Few gardeners can spare the room to accommodate this tall native species with its broad sword-like leaves and those who can, would do better to grow the soft primrose var. *bastardi* or rich golden-yellow 'Golden Queen'. Where space is limited the less vigorous 'Variegata' can be recommended, its spiky foliage being conspicuously striped with green and gold.

I. versicolor This is a shorter version of our yellow flag which hails from North America. It enjoys much the same conditions, but instead of producing bright yellow blossoms, has violet-blue flowers veined with purple and splashed gold. Its variety 'Kermesina' is even more lovely, having blooms of deep velvety plum with similar distinctive markings.

All the iris species grow readily from seed or can be divided, as is obviously essential for the named garden varieties.

Juncus effusus Soft Rush. This native species, along with most other *Juncus* species, are common inhabitants of wet pastures and marshes throughout the northern hemisphere and not particularly suited to garden conditions. Amongst the few that can be recommended, the golden varegated *J. effusus* 'Vittatus' with its 2 ft (60 cm) high needle-like foliage longitudinally striped with green and gold is unquestionably the most attractive. *Juncus effusus* 'Spiralis', on the other hand, takes the prize for being the most bizarre, with its curiously malformed stems that grow in a corkscrew-like fashion and have earned the plant the common name of corkscrew rush. Wild species of rush are easily propagated from seed, but good garden varieties have to be increased by division in the spring.

Ludwigia palustris False Loosestrife. Those who keep an aquarium will be familiar with the innumerable species of *Ludwigia* that are grown by aquarists as submerged oxygenating plants. This hardy fellow is of the same family, but with handsome spiky foliage and curious petalless flowers.

Mentha aquatica Water Mint. This strongly aromatic plant enjoys shallow water or wet mud at the poolside and when happily accommodated produces dense terminal whorls of lilac-pink flowers on slender reddish stems amongst an abundance of hairy greyish-green foliage. It is a fairly rapid grower, its probing white rhizomes running across the surface of the compost and jumping from basket to basket if given the opportunity. While a dubious proposition for the very small pool, it can be used to advantage as a foil elsewhere and is readily increased by short soft cuttings during the summer months or by division of the creeping rhizome.

Menyanthes trifoliata Bog Bean, Buck Bean. A distinctive plant for shallow water which bears decorative white fringed flowers during May above dark green trifoliate leaves, not unlike those of a broad bean. Both the leaves and the flowers are protected by a short scaly sheath situated towards the end of each sprawling olive-green rhizome and the latter, if chopped into sections each with a root attached, forms a successful means of propagation.

Figure 4.6: *Menyanthes trifoliata* — Bog Bean, Buck Bean

Mimulus luteus Musk. Although seldom a permanent resident of the pool, this lovely yellow flowered species and its brightly coloured cultivars often seed and naturalise themselves amongst other marginals, or with the gardener's help they can be perpetuated from cuttings overwintered in a cold frame. There are innumerable fine varieties and strains available, from the vivid red 'Bonfire', pastel coloured 'Monarch Strain' to the boldly spotted 'Queen's Prize' and 'Tigrinus' strains. For the rock pool or sink garden there is the tiny 'Whitecroft Scarlet', 'Highland Red' and 'Highland Pink', while the gardener looking for something out of the ordinary can be satisfied by the almost double 'Hose-in-Hose' with yellow blooms that consist of one flower inside another.

M. ringens This is really the only truly aquatic species of mimulus, a delicate looking plant with much branched slender stems and handsome narrow leaflets. It usually attains a height of 1½ ft (45 cm) and although it seldom seeds itself in the pool, it is easily raised from a spring sowing under glass or from short soft stem cuttings taken during mid-summer and rooted in a pan of mud.

Myosotis scorpioides (syn. *M. palustris*) Water Forget-me-not. During early summer this charming little native is smothered in sky-blue flowers that are almost identical to those of the familiar bedding forget-me-not. An improved form called 'Semperflorens' is even lovelier, producing fewer leaves and being less inclined to straggle across the mud. Seed raising is the most usual means of propagation although division of established plants in early spring is generally successful. Sometimes when plants are raised from seed one or two will turn out to be the not unattractive white form.

Narthecium ossifragum Bog Asphodel. A diminutive plant with a wiry creeping rhizome and small fans of reddish-green iris-like foliage amongst which are produced terminal clusters of bright yellow flowers. Very useful for the sink garden, but must be used carefully in the moderate sized pool as it really only enjoys wet conditions rather than prolonged submersion.

Peltandra virginica Arrow Arum. A handsome member of the arum family with narrow pea-green spathes amidst dark green, glossy, arrow-shaped foliage which arises from a short fleshy rootstock which readily divides to form new plants. A slightly larger species with white spathes, *P. alba*, is sometimes encountered and is equally amenable.

Pontederia cordata Pickerel Weed. This is a plant of noble proportions, producing numerous stems each consisting of an oval or lanceolate shiny green leaf and a leafy bract from which the spike of soft blue flowers emerges during August and September. It attains a height of 2 or 3 ft (60 or 90 cm). *Pontederia* can be easily increased by division of the rootstock in early spring or from seed which is sown green immediately after being gathered.

Preslia cervina A delightful little aquatic which has spreading clumps of slender erect stems densely clothed in small lanceolate leaves, crowned during late summer with stiff whorled spikes of dainty ultramarine or lilac flowers. The entire plant is strongly aromatic and happiest when growing in very shallow water. It can be easily increased from short stem cuttings taken during spring and inserted in pots of wet mud.

Ranunculus flammula Lesser Spearwort. An interesting creeping buttercup-like plant with glistening golden blossoms above dark green oval foliage which is carried on distinctive red wiry stems which root wherever they touch the soil. Easily increased by pieces of stem which root readily.

R. lingua Greater Spearwort. A tall growing species, often 3 ft (90 cm) high, with erect hollow stems well clothed with narrow dark green leaves and large golden blossoms. A natural octaploid variant, *R. lingua* 'Grandiflora', is the plant usually grown and this flowers for much of the summer.

Sagittaria japonica Arrowhead. A marginal plant of happy

Figure 4.7:
Ranunculus lingua
'Grandiflora' —
Spearwort with
Nymphaea

disposition with broad arrow-shaped foliage which arises from large turions or winter buds. These are almost potato-like in appearance and are popularly known as duck potatoes, wild ducks delighting in digging them up and eating them whenever given the opportunity. The flower spike has tiered whorls of white three-petalled flowers with bright golden centres which in the cultivar 'Flore-Pleno' are replaced by myriad tiny petals which give the individual blossoms the appearance of tiny powder puffs.

S. latifolia This is the largest arrowhead usually cultivated, an imposing character some 4 or 5 ft (1 m 20 cm or 1 m 50 cm) high with soft green awl-shaped leaves and sprays of snow-white flowers. Both double and hairy leafed forms occasionally appear in cultivation.

S. sagittifolia Common Arrowhead. This is very similar to *S. japonica*, but with more acutely cut foliage and white flowers with black and crimson centres. Like all the other arrowheads, this is propagated by gathering the winter buds and planting them individually.

Saururus cernuus Lizards' Tail. A rather bizarre, but nevertheless attractive little aquatic for shallow water. It produces clumps of heart-shaped foliage which often takes on bright autumnal tints, particularly under acid growing conditions. The strange nodding sprays of creamy-white flowers are produced above the leaves during July and August. It is easily increased by division in the spring.

Scirpus lacustris Bulrush. The true bulrush as opposed to the reedmace, which is most people's idea of a bulrush, is an extremely useful plant for shallow water. It produces stiff dark green needle-like leaves from short hardy creeping rhizomes and during June and July is bedecked with pendant tassels of crowded reddish-brown flowers.

S. tabernaemontani Glaucous Bulrush. This is a superior garden plant in all respects to our native bulrush. Not only does it generally grow taller, attaining a height of some 5 ft (1 m 50 cm), but has beautiful slender foliage of steely-grey with a conspicuous mealy bloom. Although an excellent subject in its own right, it has given rise to the quite remarkable zebra rush, *S.t.* 'Zebrinus', a popular mutant in which the stems are alternately barred with green and white. It seldom grows more than 3 ft (90 cm) high and does best when allowed to colonise very shallow water. When occasional plain green stems are produced these should be removed before they outgrow the more desirable variegated portion. No such problem occurs with the variety 'Albe-

scens', a plant of uncertain origin, but one with stout upright
stems of a glowing sulphurous-white conspicuously marked
with thin green longitudinal stripes. These arise from clumps
of thick creeping rhizomes which are not reliably hardy in
the north of the country and often protected with a light
covering of straw or bracken litter. Both *S. lacustris* and *S.
tabernaemontani* and its forms are propagated by division of
the rhizome when the young shoots show signs of active
growth during early spring.

Sparganium ramosum Bur Reed. A rather coarse rush-like
plant which has bright green foliage and clustered heads of
brownish-green flowers. These give rise to a spiky seed head
rather like a small teasel. Should be introduced to the lined
pool with caution, for the bur reed has sharp creeping
rhizomes which are capable of puncturing a polythene pool
liner. It can be propagated by division of the rootstocks
during early spring.

Typha angustifolia Reedmace. This is the narrow-leafed
version of the vigorous native *T. latifolia*, the other species
to which the name reedmace, and more incorrectly bulrush,
is popularly appended. Although looking very impressive
when growing along streamsides and around large ponds in
the countryside, these much loved aquatics should be
regarded with caution when contemplated for the garden
pool, for they attain a height of at least 6 ft (1 m 80 cm) and
spread rapidly by means of thick white rhizomes.

T. laxmannii (syn. *T. stenophylla*) This is a much more
restrained character, seldom attaining more than 3 ft (90
cm) in height, and producing typical well proportioned
chocolate brown poker-like heads above slender willowy
foliage.

T. minima This splendid little plant produces masses of short
fat brown flower spikes amongst a waving sea of grassy
foliage. As it seldom grows more than $1\frac{1}{2}$ ft (45 cm) high it
can be successfully accommodated in the tiniest pool. As
with the large vigorous species, *T. minima* can be increased
by division in the early spring.

Veronica beccabunga Brooklime. This is the only truly aquatic
member of this popular family of garden plants. In common
with its terrestial cousins it has dark blue flowers with white
eyes, but unlike the more familiar kinds carries these in the
axils of the leaves rather than in bold terminal spikes. While
not a spectacular plant, the brooklime is exceedingly useful
for masking the harsh edges of the pool, tolerating moist
conditions on land as well as spreading its trailing stems

across the surface of the water, providing shade for the fish and its hanging roots a suitable deposition for spawn. This is one of the few aquatic plants that is best replaced annually. Strong young shoots readily root in trays of mud in early spring and make much better plants than their parents would if left for a further year.

CHAPTER 5

Submerged and Floating Plants

Submerged oxygenating plants, in conjunction with floating aquatics, take a leading role in the maintenance of clear water in the garden pool. For not only do they compete with the lower forms of plant life such as slimes and algae for mineral salts in the water, but also provide surface shade which makes life difficult for any primitive plants that try to dwell beneath.

Planting
Submerged
Plants

A generally accepted formula for planting a new pool so that harmony and a healthy balance exists at the outset, is that one-third of the total surface area of the pool, excluding the shallow marginal shelves, should be clothed with floating foliage. This need not necessarily be composed entirely of floating plants, for waterlilies and other deep water aquatics make a considerable contribution in this direction with their floating foliage.

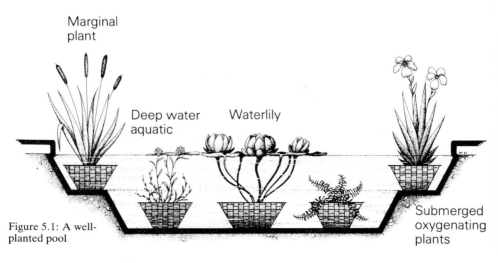

Marginal
plant

Deep water
aquatic

Waterlily

Submerged
oxygenating
plants

Figure 5.1: A well-
planted pool

Submerged oxygenating plants are purchased as bunches of cuttings and should be planted at a density of one bunch to every square foot of surface area of the pool, excluding the margins, to ensure relatively clear water from the outset. That is not to say that they should be distributed checkerboard style all over the floor of the pool, for they will perform their function quite adequately if concentrated in two or three containers spread about the pool. It is the total volume of plant material that is important. Although submerged oxygenating plants are sold as bunches of cuttings fastened together with lead strips, and seem to be clinging precariously to life, once introduced to the pool roots are rapidly initiated.

When planting submerged oxygenating plants do not merely toss them into the water as some nurserymen suggest, for while it is true that the plants gain most of their nourishment directly from the water, they cannot prosper unless anchored securely to the bottom. In an established pool where there is an accumulation of mulm and debris on the pool floor this method of dropping the plants into the water and allowing the lead weight to take them root down to the bottom can be successful.

While submerged plants do benefit from being anchored to the bottom, it does not follow that they have to be planted in a huge container of soil. Small flower pots or even deep plastic

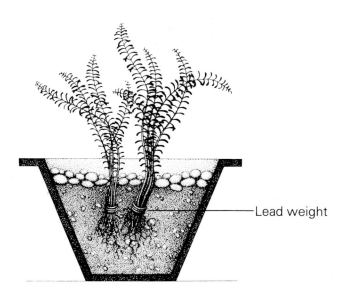

Lead weight

Figure 5.2: Submerged oxygenating plants planted with buried lead weights

Figure 5.3: Planting oxygenating plants. The basket has been prepared as for deep water aquatics (see pp. 21-2)

Figure 5.4: Placing a basket of oxygenating plants in the pool

seed trays can be used with great success, and the preparation of the planting medium and containers should be the same as described for the deep water aquatics (see pp. 21-2). The rooting medium can be fine pea gravel, although most gardeners agree that a good stiff loam topped off with fine shingle is really the best. No matter which medium or container is used, the planting technique is the same, the lead strip being left attached to the bunch of cuttings and buried intact. If the lead strip is left exposed it rots through the stems and the cuttings come floating to the surface. Floating plants are easily dealt with, as all gain nourishment directly from the water and merely need throwing into the water when received from the nursery.

Apium inundatum Water Celery. This is one of the few submerged plants that is sold as a rooted plant rather than a bunch of cuttings. It has fresh delicately cut foliage and crowded heads of white flowers above the surface of the water.

Callitriche hermaphroditica (syn. *C. autumnalis*) Autumnal Starwort. This is a totally submerged species of starwort with evergreen cress-like foliage that is considered a delicacy by most coldwater fish.

C. platycarpa (syn. *C. verna*) A most useful species for shallower water, where it will not only produce its dense underwater cress-like foliage, but terminal whorls of bright green elliptical floating foliage. Another plant beloved of goldfish, but only of summer duration, the foliage disappearing completely during the winter.

C. stagnalis A native starwort with oval leaves of luxuriant bright green that often disappear once the plant has fruited. All three starworts are easily increased by short cuttings or division. The first two species are better known in the trade by their synonyms, despite the fact that botanists updated their names many years ago.

Ceratophyllum demersum Hornwort, Coontail. Only the minutest of botanical details separate this from *C. submersum*, so to the gardener they are equally useful and aesthetically identical. Both are valuable plants for difficult pools preferring deep cool water and are not unduly affected by shade. They both have dark green bristly foliage arranged in dense whorls around slender brittle stems. In early spring these become rooted to the pool floor, but as the summer progresses they float to the surface, the stem towards the terminal buds thickening and breaking off, leaving the upper portions to sink to the bottom as turions or winter buds.

Chara aspera Stonewort. This is only one of many species of stonewort to be found in garden pools. Loosely speaking they are intermediate between higher submerged plants and filamentous algae, being of a thick hairy appearance and rooting strongly to the pool floor. They vary in colour from pale green to a bluish-green and generally possess an offensive odour that has been likened to that attributed to

Submerged
Oxygenating
Plants

Figure 5.5:
*Ceratophyllum
demersum* —
Hornwort, Coontail

57

male cats. Apart from their very obvious oxygenating benefits, the stoneworts are noted as being one of the few plant groups that can extract lime from water. If a plant is removed and dried in the sun a chalky deposit will soon become evident. Stoneworts usually find their own way into garden pools, but *Chara aspera* is often bunched and sold commercially.

Eleocharis acicularis Hair Grass. Another submerged plant that is sold as a rooted plant rather than bunched cuttings. It is a delicate carpeting plant with grassy foliage, so fine that it looks like seedling lawn grass. Often used in cold water aquaria, this is absolutely hardy.

Elodea canadensis Canadian Pondweed. Sadly this species has a bad reputation for being unruly and swamping the pool, when in fact it is really quite restrained and one of the most versatile oxygenating plants the pool owner can grow. It received its bad name at the end of the last century when it was introduced to Europe and rapidly spread, choking canals and waterways and making them virtually unnavigable. Fortunately it died out after several years leaving a much less pernicious form in its place; it is a possibility that the vigour of the plant was related to its sex and that the form now available to gardeners is the female clone. *Elodea canadensis* has dark green curved lance-like leaflets borne in whorls around long branching stems and tiny floating lilac flowers with trailing thread-like stalks. Easily increased by bunches of cuttings taken at any time during the growing season and planted as described earlier.

Fontinalis antipyretica Willow Moss. A handsome evergreen native with dark green mossy foliage that thrives equally well in sun or shade and is tolerant of moving water. Together with the more diminutive *F. gracilis* this species provides an excellent spawning ground for goldfish. Neither enjoys alkaline conditions.

Figure 5.6:
*Fontinalis
antipyretica* —
Willow Moss

Tillaea recurva (syn. *Crassula recurva*). One of the most neglected submerged oxygenating plants until recent years when it was realised how valuable it could be in clearing green water in established pools. Unlike many other submerged plants it can be lifted in clumps, instantly forming a 'mature' plant. If planted in a pool that is consistently green, in thick well rooted clumps, it can almost be guaranteed to clear the water within a month. It has hard cress-like foliage which during mid-summer is littered with tiny white axillary flowers.

Azolla caroliniana Fairy Moss. This is a little floating fern which, with the closely allied *A. filiculoides*, is one of the few floating carpeting plants that can be safely introduced to the pool. It provides a thick lacy carpet of floating bluish-green or, in the autumn, brilliant crimson congested foliage. Although perfectly hardy in most parts of the British Isles, it is desirable to keep a portion of these plants in a frost-free place during the winter months, for when left outside they form overwintering bodies which disappear, not to return to the surface until the water has started to warm up. This is often too late for them to act as effective surface cover, whereas if a portion of the plant (that has been kept actively growing) is introduced into the pool, it will spread rapidly during late April and have the desired effect.

Hydrocharis morsus-ranae Frogbit. The frogbit is a local native plant that in general appearance looks like a very tiny waterlily with its floating rosettes of kidney-shaped leaves. The white three-petalled flowers show clearly that it is not related to the waterlily, but rather the water soldier, *Stratiotes aloides*, with which in every other respect it seems to have little in common. *Hydrocharis* forms turions which overwinter on the pool floor. They disappear around the end of September and do not reappear until the middle of May, so it is advisable to remove a few plants and put them in a large jar of water with a generous layer of soil on the bottom, so that floating cover can be provided early in the spring before algae becomes too troublesome.

Lemna trisulca Ivy-leafed Duckweed. Most of the duckweeds are too troublesome to consider for the average garden pool, spreading rapidly and soon obscuring the water entirely from view. The more amenable *L. trisulca* is a dark green crispy foliage plant which floats just beneath the surface of the water and rarely causes any problems. It

Floating Plants

61

produces minute greenish flowers, but is grown for its decorative foliage.

Stratiotes aloides Water Soldier. An interesting native which has large rosettes of dark green spiny foliage reminiscent of a pineapple top. Its creamy-white flowers are produced in the same manner as those of a strawberry plant.

Trapa natans Water Chestnut. A handsome plant with neat rosettes of dark green rhomboidal floating leaves and creamy-white axillary flowers. Although an annual, the black horned nuts, which give it its common name, are produced freely throughout late summer and germinate freely each spring. Some gardeners are rather nervous of risking the seeds in the open pond for the winter and so harvest them. If stored in wet sphagnum moss and germinated in early spring in a jar of water, good strong plants will be produced. The most important thing to remember is that the seeds die if dried out.

Utricularia minor Lesser Bladderwort. This is the smaller growing species of our native bladderworts. Its wand-like flower spikes are held above the water and bear tiny pouched flowers of soft primrose which arise from a tangled mass of delicate lacy olive-green foliage which, in common with all the other bladderworts, is interspersed with tiny bladders which capture minute aquatic insect life.

U. vulgaris Greater Bladderwort. From a tangled mass of filigree foliage showy spires of blossoms are produced during July. These are bright golden-yellow and look very much like those of an antirrhinum but are more sparsely distributed along the flower spike. The intermediate Bladderwort, *U. intermedia*, is more or less intermediate between *U. minor* and *U. vulgaris*, differing only in that it produces bladders in colourless foliage, although it has green deeply dissected foliage as well.

CHAPTER 6

Bog Garden and Stream

A bog garden is a natural extension of the pool in which moisture-loving plants can be grown. It should be appreciated at the outset though that these are not true aquatics and will not tolerate waterlogged conditions, but revel in damp soil which may become flooded occasionally, and thus are also suitable for streamside planting.

Constructing a bog garden is not difficult if provision is made for it when the pool is constructed. Introducing a bog garden afterwards is fraught with difficulties unless one is very practical and imaginative. When a pool is being constructed using a liner there is no problem; all that needs to be done is to order the liner larger than required for the pool and incorporate it at the edge as if it were a spreading shallow pool about a foot (30 cm) deep. A retaining wall of loose bricks or stones should be spread across the border of the pool proper and the bog garden, the latter being filled with an equal parts mixture of coarse peat and heavy soil over a layer of gravel. This ensures a moisture-retentive medium, but allows excess water to drain away from the roots. Water from the pool percolates through the barrier and ensures that the soil is kept damp, this latter being maintained an inch (2.5 cm) or so above mean water level.

An extension to a concrete pool can be made in a similar manner using concrete as a lining material, although pool liners of PVC or rubber can be used effectively to create a independent bog garden adjacent to a concrete pool or pre-shaped structure. The only problem with this form of construction is that the bog garden has to be maintained separately from the pool, yet must give the appearance of being an integral part of it.

63

The Stream

Few gardeners can create a stream and make it look convincing, unless on a grand scale. However, many do inherit such a natural feature in their garden and find it difficult to cope with, for it can be a turbulent fury during winter and yet reduced to a trickle during summer, so the choice of plant material has to be considered very carefully. Of course many things can be done with a stream apart from planting. Cascades can be created and pools filled, but great care must be taken when restricting or altering the flow, for if the stream is of minor local importance it is easy to flood inadvertently a neighbour's garden or one's own.

The only safe way in which the flow of a stream may be checked or diverted is by the addition of stepping stones strategically placed so that they create a calm area near one bank where truly aquatic subjects may be grown. Where a stream is wide or deep a bridge may be necessary to enable it to be crossed, or even when this is not essential a well-made structure in rustic timber or stone will make an attractive focal point. Stepping stones can also be used, but these should be carefully selected as they must be level, reasonably smooth and of stone that is not going to be shaled by frost.

Planting a Bog Garden

Unlike true aquatic plants, those of the bog garden or streamside must be planted during the traditional planting season which extends from late September until mid-March. Generally they are border plants of an herbaceous nature which, although needing plenty of moisture to grow prolifically, cannot tolerate standing water. Once established they require little care apart from routine weed and pest control, and the tidying up of superfluous foliage immediately the frost has killed it in order to deprive aquatic insect pests of a winter refuge. Most bog garden plants require lifting and dividing every third or fourth year in order to maintain flower size and general vigour.

Bog Garden Plants

Aconitum napellus Monkshood. A well-known cottage garden plant that produces tolerable flower spikes under ordinary border conditions, but which is really at home in the bog garden. Of somewhat delphinium-like appearance, it has towering spikes of dark blue hooded blossoms 5 ft (1 m 50 cm) or more high and handsome dark green glossy foliage. 'Bressingham Spire' is a shorter growing variety which is ideal for the small garden, while *A. napellus bicolor* has striking blossoms of blue and white.

Ajuga reptans Bugle. The most useful member of a family of dense creeping herbaceous subjects that are invaluable for growing in the soil surrounding the pool so that they can tumble over the edge and disguise its harshness. The common bugle is not worth considering in the small garden, but its cultivated varieties are most attractive. 'Purpurea' has purplish-bronze leaves, while the foliage of 'Multicolor' is pinkish-buff with cream variegations on a green background. All have spikes of dark blue flowers some 6 in (15 cm) high that smother the plants from late May until July.

Anthericum liliago St Bernard's Lily. A lovely summer flowering perennial with grassy foliage and 2 ft (60 cm) high spikes of pure white trumpet-shaped blossoms.

A. liliastrum major St Bruno Lily. Very similar to *A. liliago*, but with larger, bolder, trumpet-shaped blossoms.

Aruncus sylvester (syn. *Spiraea aruncus*) Goat's Beard. A towering plant of *Astilbe*-like appearance with frothy plumes of creamy-white flowers 4 or 5 ft (1 m 20 or 1 m 50 cm) high. The leaves are pale green and deeply cut and lobed, while the stems are hard and green, and somewhat bamboo-like in appearance. A dwarf form called 'Kneiffi' is of similar appearance, but with finely divided foliage and seldom exceeds 3 ft (90 cm) in height. Both flower during July and early August and are easily increased by division during the dormant season.

Asclepias incarnata Swamp Milkweed. A splendid, but much neglected summer flowering waterside plant which produces stout leafy stems and crowded heads of rose-pink flowers. There is a white form too, and both are easily increased by division during early spring.

Aster puniceus Swamp Aster. This could really be described as a moisture-loving Michaelmas daisy for it flowers during September with typical lilac blossoms, a little smaller than one might expect, but in perfect conformity, for it is a short growing plant which seldom exceeds 3 ft (90 cm) in height. It is readily propagated by division, but can be raised from seed as well.

Astilbe hybrids False Goat's Beard. The popular garden hybrids of this lovely family of moisture-loving perennials are a complex union of *Astilbe astilboides*, *A. japonica*, *A. sinensis* and *A. thunbergii*. None of the species is worth growing in the decorative garden when there is such an array of hardy beauties that they have sired. For instance there is the bright crimson 'Fanal', also 'Red Sentinel' and the delicious salmon-pink 'Peach Blossom' as well as the icy-white 'White Gloria'. Apart from these four, there are probably another twenty or thirty cultivars of equal merit, all with handsome clumps of pale green foliage surmounted by brightly coloured feathery spikes of flowers. Heights vary from as little as 6 in (15 cm) in the dwarf *crispa* varieties like 'Lilliput' or 'Perkeo', to 4 ft (1 m 20 cm) in some of the more vigorous hybrids. All are easily increased from division in the spring and those of modest stature can be utilised for forcing in the cool greenhouse to provide an early show of colour. This has little effect upon their subsequent performance outside providing that they are not forced every year but given an opportunity to rest.

Bupthalmum speciosum A strange daisy-like plant with large drooping yellow flowers during June and early July, and hairy aromatic foliage. Under favourable conditions it reaches a height of 4 ft (1 m 20 cm) and is therefore not so useful for the small garden. It is quickly raised from seed and can also be divided during the dormant season.

Cardamine pratensis Cuckoo Flower. A pretty spring-flowering waterside perennial with single rosy-lilac flowers above tufts of pale green ferny foliage. There is a double form called *flore-plena* and this is even more attractive. Neither grow more than 1 ft (30 cm) tall and the species can be easily raised from seed, the double form from division.

Eupatorium purpureum Joe-Pye-Weed. A rather coarse-leafed perennial with crowded heads of purple flowers on stems 4 ft (1 m 20 cm) high. Ideal for streamside planting, providing colour in late summer and early autumn. Can be increased by division or seed sown during early spring.

Euphorbia palustris A moisture-loving member of the spurge family with lush green foliage and large yellow-green flower heads during early summer. It seldom grows more than 3 ft (90 cm) high and is best propagated from division when the young shoots are emerging during early spring.

Filipendula hexapetala Dropwort. An attractive fern-leafed species of meadow sweet with characteristic creamy-white flowers on stems some 2 ft (60 cm) high. There is also a charming fully double form *flore-pleno*.

F. palmata This has delicately poised 3 ft (90 cm) stems of pale pink flowers above spreading bright green leaves.

F. ulmaria Meadow Sweet. Our native meadow sweet is a most attractive bog garden subject, flaunting frothy spires of creamy-white blossoms above handsome deeply cut foliage. The double form is the best one to grow for flowers, and the golden-leafed 'Aurea' has the most striking foliage. In common with the other *Filipendulas*, our common meadow sweet and its varieties are easily propagated by division in the spring.

Gunnera manicata Looking rather like a giant rhubarb, it has enormous kidney-shaped leaves 5 ft (1 m 50 cm) or more across with deeply indented margins and undersides and leaf stalks that are liberally sprinkled with unpleasant bristly hairs. It has a strange branched flower spike like a huge red-green bottle brush that may be up to 3 ft (90 cm) high. This arises from a thick creeping rhizome that is densely clothed in brown papery scales, and during winter looks rather like a reclining bear. Coming from Brazil, this imposing bog garden plant is not reliably hardy in the colder parts of Britain and the USA, so a covering of straw, bracken or, with established plants, their own frost blackened leaves, will be sufficient to prevent a sharp frost scorching their overwintering buds. Although a giant of a plant, it is frequently offered by nurseries and is so well known that it could not conceivably be omitted from any survey of bog garden plants. Propagation is from division of the crowns in early spring or from seed sown immediately it ripens.

Hemerocallis hybrids Day Lily. The modern daylilies, of which

Figure 6.1:
Hemerocallis 'Pink Charm' — Day Lily

there are literally hundreds, are of complex origin, and derived principally from unions between *Hemerocallis fulva*, *H. lilio-asphodelus* and *H. flava*, with the occasional intervention of two or three others. This has resulted in many fine hybrids, especially from the United States, that it is difficult to come to a decision over selection. Of the older and well tried cultivars, the lemon-yellow 'Hyperion', orange 'Mikado' and aptly named 'Pink Charm' are difficult to surpass. All *Hemerocallis* have narrow arching strap-like leaves in large tufts and these support narrow wiry flower stems with large brightly coloured trumpet-like blossoms. Each flower lasts but a day, but as there are always plenty of buds to follow, flowering continues from June through to the end of July. They are all easily propagated by division in early spring when their vigorous young shoots are just emerging.

Hosta fortunei This is one of the larger plantain lilies with handsome plain green leaves and attractive spikes of funnel-shaped lilac flowers.

H. glauca (syn. *H. sieboldii*) An even larger species with large glaucous, almost heart-shaped leaves 6 in (15 cm) wide and 1 ft (30 cm) long and spikes of off-white bell-shaped blossoms. The cultivar 'Robusta' is larger in every respect.

H. lancifolia As its name suggests this green leafed species has long lance-shaped foliage which during July is surmounted by erect sprays of lilac blossoms. The cultivar 'Fortis' is larger in every respect, 'Aurea' has lovely golden foliage and the hybrid 'Thomas Hogg' which boasts *H. lancifolia* in its parentage, produces plain green leaves with a white marginal band.

H. undulata medio-variegata Despite having the most appalling name of any plantain lily, this is probably the most popular and attractive variety commonly available. It is a smallish plant, no more than 1 ft (30 cm) high with slightly twisted or undulate leaves in a complex mixture of cream, white and green.

All hostas are readily propagated by division immediately the succulent spear-like growths appear during early spring. The species can be raised from seed, but this gives the best results when sown ripe directly from the plant.

Iris aurea A tall growing, robust and much neglected species for the bog garden. Attaining a height of 4 ft (1 m 20 cm) or more, this displays perfectly formed blossoms of intense golden-yellow. Will grow in the most hostile of conditions and is an excellent companion for *I. ochroleuca*.

I. bulleyana A charming little blue-flowered Chinese species with bold tufts of grassy foliage.

I. chrysographes Preferring a sunny position, this lovely little fellow, no more than 2 ft (60 cm) high, has blossoms of rich velvety purple and somewhat broader leaves than *I. bulleyana*.

I. kaempferi Japanese Clematis Flowered Iris. This beautiful swamp iris has tufts of broad grassy foliage surmounted by clematis-like flowers which resemble exotic tropical butterflies at rest. Some of the best varieties are 'Blue Heaven' with rich purple-blue velvety petals marked with yellow, the fully double pale rose-lavender 'Landscape at Dawn' and deep violet 'Mandarin'. For gardeners who want something really spectacular there is the magnificent giant flowered 'Higo' strain with colossal vividly coloured blossoms 8 in (20 cm) across or the more refined 'Tokyo' strain with beautifully sculptured blooms in many colours. For foliage effect *I. kaempferi* 'Variegata' is hard to beat, for this more modest character has boldly striped leaves of cream and green, and small violet-blue flowers. All the clematis-flowered iris are at their best during June and early July and none grows any taller than 2½ ft (75 cm) and so are excellent for even the smallest bog garden. Good mixtures of *I. kaempferi* can be raised from seed, but the variegated kind and the named varieties must be increased by division in early spring or immediately after they have finished flowering. Unlike most other irises, these demand an acid soil.

I. ochroleuca Growing to 5 ft (1 m 50 cm), this bold yellow and white flowered species is the best for a difficult soil or situation. Not only is it attractive in flower, but the emerging spears of glaucous foliage have a lovely bloom on them very much like that of grapes.

I. sibirica This race of iris are of similar habit to *I. kaempferi*, but with less spectacular blossoms and an easier going disposition, not resenting alkaline conditions like their Oriental cousins. *Iris sibirica* itself is a rather modest character with clumps of grassy foliage and pale blue flowers. However, its hybrids are more striking, particularly the sky-blue 'Perry's Blue' and deep violet 'Ottawa', 'Snow Queen' is pure white, 'Emperor' deep violet-blue, while 'Perry's Pygmy' as its name suggests is a much shorter kind with deep violet blossoms.

All the iris cultivars can be increased by division immediately after flowering or in the early spring just as the spears of foliage are appearing. The species can also be raised easily from seed.

Ligularia clivorum This is a lovely member of the daisy family which is not too far removed from that bane of all gardeners, the groundsel. It is not at all pernicious though, producing violet-green heart-shaped leaves and huge mop heads of droopy orange flowers. A splendid plant for the late summer garden, it is only surpassed by its cultivars 'Othello' with orange blossoms and deep purplish foliage, the vivid 'Orange Queen' and pale yellow flowered 'Desdemona'. Although *Ligularia* is easily raised from seed, the resulting plants are very variable, so division in early spring must be employed. This is essential for the named varieties in any event.

Lobelia cardinalis A perennial species that is not reliably hardy in all parts of the country. It has vivid red blossoms on bold spikes amongst bright green foliage and grows to a height of 3 ft (90 cm). It is a wise precaution to overwinter a few rosettes of the dormant plant in a frame or cold greenhouse.

L. fulgens Often confused with *L. cardinalis*, this tougher perennial has the same bright red blossoms, but contrasting foliage of a rich beetroot colour.

L. vedrariensis An interesting lobelia with mid-green foliage flushed with purple and intense violet flowers. Like the other two, a later summer flowering plant which can be readily increased from seed or division.

Lysichitum americanum Skunk Cabbage. A member of the Arum family, this produces bright yellow spathes in April before its large cabbagy leaves appear. The individual spathes are up to 2 ft (60 cm) high and the succeeding foliage in excess of 3 ft (90 cm).

L. camtschatense A slightly smaller white version of the preceding. Both species are readily increased from seed sown immediately it ripens.

Lysimachia nummularia Creeping Jenny. This is an evergreen carpeting plant that is ideal for masking the edge of the pool or providing an attractive ground cover between taller growing marsh plants in the bog garden. It seldom exceeds 2 in (5 cm) in height and is studded with starry buttercup-like flowers during June and July. The cultivar 'Aurea' has bright yellow foliage.

L. punctata This vigorous plant, some 2 or 3 ft (60-90 cm) high has similar blossoms to creeping Jenny, but borne in whorls on stout spikes amongst rugged downy foliage.

Figure 6.2:
*Lysichitum
americanum* —
Skunk Cabbage

Figure 6.3:
*Lysichitum
camtschatense* —
Skunk Cabbage

Lythrum salicaria Purple Loosestrife. A native plant with bushy stems 4 ft (1 m 20 cm) high and slender spikes of deep rose-purple blooms. Improved cultivars include 'The Beacon', 'Lady Sackville' and 'Robert' which range in colour from purple, through rose-pink, to pink.

L. virgatum A smaller version with dark green leaves and purple blossoms which rarely grows more than 2½ ft (45 cm) high. 'Rose Queen' and 'Dropmore Purple' are two garden varieties that are well worth growing. The species can be increased from seed while the named varieties are propagated by cuttings or careful division.

Mimulus cardinalis Cardinal Monkey Flower. Unlike the species mentioned in the chapter on marginal plants, this does not enjoy standing in water, although it does respond to damp conditions. It has attractive hoary foliage and brilliant scarlet-orange flowers and, although not winter hardy in some parts of Britain, is easily overwintered as cuttings in an unheated frame. Seed sown during early spring provides an alternative method of propagation.

Parnassia palustris Grass of Parnassus. This is a beautiful rare native for the keen gardener, for it is almost as difficult to grow as it is beautiful. Few gardeners on seeing it for the first time would deny themselves the challenge. It grows best near moving water and for that reason should be positioned in the splash of a stream or cascade. An inveterate lime-hater, it bears its charming snow-white flowers, occasionally blotched with apple-green, on slender stems amongst neat clumps of heart-shaped leaves. It can be propagated from seed, or division if you are prepared to risk disturbing the plant.

Peltiphyllum peltatum (syn. *Saxifraga peltata*) Umbrella Plant. This striking Californian native should find a home beside every pool, for its stout stems bear immense leaves of a bronzy-green hue which are often 1 ft (30 cm) in diameter. They are handsomely lobed and toothed and preceded in early spring by globular heads of rose-coloured flowers on sturdy stems 1½ ft (45 cm) high. It can be raised from seed, but division of the fleshy rhizome in early spring brings quicker results.

Petasites japonicus Butterbur. This is one of several species of *Petasites* offered by nurserymen for the bog garden but should be avoided unless one has plenty of room. While it flowers very early with crowded heads of white flowers on neat short stems and is invaluable on that account, it also produces large unwieldy cabbage-like foliage later in the season, 5 ft (1 m 50 cm) high.

Phormium tenax New Zealand Flax. A remarkable bog garden plant with bold sword-like foliage of metallic green and stout stems bearing numerous curious red and yellow flowers. Its varieties *atropurpurea* with reddish-purple foliage and *variegata* with leaves of green, yellow and white are even more outstanding, as are many of the modern named cultivars. However, a number of these seem to be rather unreliable in the winter and are best avoided unless one lives in the southern half of Britain. The species can be raised from seed, but the varieties and cultivars must be propagated by careful division in the spring.

Primula Part of this lovely genus of garden plants is excellent for the bog garden, flourishing equally well in sun or partial shade, and when planted in bold drifts presenting a picture of unrivalled splendour. They all form rosettes of distinctive foliage from which arise slender stems bearing richly coloured flowers arranged in globular heads or tiered whorls.

Primula 'Asthore Hybrids' Handsome plants with whorled tiers of flowers in white, pink and peach shades during May. (1½ ft (45 cm))

P. aurantiaca This is one of the first candelabra primulas to flower during early May with tiers of bright orange blossoms. (2½ ft (75 cm))

P. beesiana A candelabra-type with rich rosy-purple flowers during June and July. (2 ft (60 cm))

P. bulleyana This is a candelabra-type with orange-yellow flowers during June and July. (2½ ft (75 cm))

Figure 6.4: *Primula bulleyana*

73

P. chungensis This little gem from Yunnan has pale orange blossoms during June and seldom exceeds 1 ft (30 cm) in height.

P. denticulata Drumstick Primula. This flowers during March and April with rounded heads of blue or lilac flowers on short stout stems. The variety *alba* is white and *cashmireana* has lilac-purple blooms and mealy foliage. (1 ft (30 cm))

Figure 6.5: *Primula denticulata*

Figure 6.6: *Primula pulverulenta*

P. florindae Himalayan Cowslip. The common name describes this plant perfectly for it looks in all respects like our native cowslip, but many times larger, reaching a height of 3 ft (90 cm) under favourable conditions.

P. helodoxa A strong growing species with stout stems and

waterlilies having been awarded the Silver Medal of the Society of American Florists. Its large, deep pink, sweetly scented blossoms are held high above the water. They have yellow stamens tipped with pink and green sepals with light pink interiors. The young flower buds are green with conspicuous purple stripes, and the large purplish-green leaves splashed with red beneath. ($1\frac{1}{2}$-$2\frac{1}{2}$ ft (45-75 cm))

'Green Smoke' This extraordinary recent introduction has chartreuse petals shading to light blue at the tips. The leaves are slightly scalloped, bronzy-green with a bronze speckling. ($1\frac{1}{2}$-$2\frac{1}{2}$ ft (47-75 cm))

'Independence' This has rich rose-pink flowers and green foliage with a reddish infusion. It is strongly viviparous and a good tub plant. ($1\frac{1}{2}$-$2\frac{1}{2}$ ft (45-75 cm))

'Leading Lady' A very fragrant, almost semi-double variety, which bears huge peach-coloured blossoms that open flat, and are held above large, deep green scalloped leaves with distinctive brown freckling. Although rather large for tub culture, this is worth considering in situations where artificial lighting is necessary as it is one of the few cultivars with flowers that remain open in artificial light. ($2\frac{1}{2}$-$3\frac{1}{2}$ ft (75 cm-1 m))

'Margaret Mary' An excellent miniature blue variety for tub or aquarium culture. The tiny starry blossoms are scarcely an inch (2.5 cm) across and have golden stamens. The leaves are 2 or 3 in (5-8 cm) across, dark green above, light brown beneath. It is possible to have this variety in flower all the year round, but it does benefit from a brief resting period. This is one of the most exciting developments in waterlily breeding in recent years, and is viviparous. (1 ft (30 cm))

'Midnight' A strange variety with small, rich-purple flowers consisting of several large broad, outer petals and a cluster of small modified petals around a tiny golden centre. It is deliciously scented. The small dark green leaves are flecked with brown, deep purple beneath. (1-2 ft (30-60 cm))

'Mrs George H. Pring' Another exceptional cultivar recognised by the Society of American Florists with a silver medal. It has very fragrant, stellate, creamy-white flowers some 10 in (25 cm) across with yellow stamens. Its large green leaves are occasionally daubed with reddish-brown and have purplish reverses. ($1\frac{1}{2}$-$2\frac{1}{2}$ ft (45-75 cm))

'Panama Pacific' The buds of this cultivar open a purplish-blue but turn rich reddish-purple when the blossoms are fully expanded. It has bronze-green leaves with reddish veins. A strongly viviparous hybrid which is almost hardy and therefore useful as a summer inhabitant of the outdoor pool. (1½-2½ ft (45-75 cm))

'Patricia' A small growing crimson flowered variety with small, pale green leaves. It is viviparous and ideal for tub culture. (1-1½ ft (30-45 cm))

'Pride of Winterhaven' One of the latest and most outstanding cultivars from America. Very compact and free-flowering with stellate blossoms of rich fuchsia-lavender (1½-2½ ft (45-75 cm))

'St Louis' The large, stellate, canary-yellow blossoms have golden stamens. The pea-green leaves are faintly spotted with brown when young. (1½-2½ ft (45-75 cm))

Figure 7.2:
Nymphaea 'Pride of Winterhaven'

Night Blooming

Nymphaea amazonum (*N. ampla* of the nursery trade) This has large, sweetly scented, creamy-white flowers about 3 in (8 cm) across with thick velvety petals and cream stamens. The sepals are dark green with apple-green interiors. The handsome oval leaves are green spotted with brown above, reddish-brown spotted black beneath. This is one of the easiest waterlilies to raise from seed. (1½-2 ft (45-60 cm))

N. lotus White Nile Lotus. The deliciously scented pure-white flowers are tinged with pink and up to 8 in (20 cm) across.

Caltha palustris

Glyceria aquatica 'Variegata'

Matteucia struthiopteris

Butomus umbellatus

Lythrum salicaria

Caltha palustris 'Flore Pleno' Double Marsh Marigold

Iris kaempferi   *Lysichitum camtschatcense*

Onoclea sensibilis

Houttuynia cordata 'Plena'

Osmunda regalis

Mimulus luteus

Ranunculus lingua

Lysichitum americanum

Veronica beccabunga

Iris versicolor 'Kermesina' with *Glyceria aquatica* 'Variegata'

Nymphaea 'Escarboucle'

Nymphaea alba

Nelumbo nucifera

submerged oxygenating plant for either cool or tropical conditions. It is easily increased by short stem cuttings which can be bunched together and merely pushed into the rooting medium.

Heteranthera graminea Water Stargrass. An attractive little submerged oxygenating plant that calls to mind *Egeria densa*, but unlike that plant bears its leaflets alternatively on either side of the stem rather than in whorls. The closely allied *H. zosteraefolia*, is almost identical; but whereas *H. graminea* produces tiny pale yellow floating blossoms, this has flowers of soft blue. Propagation is by division of the clumps of foliage.

Hygrophila polysperma This is a broad-leafed submerged plant which does not look unlike *Ludwigia*. The foliage is bright green and borne on scrambling red or purplish stems. It is a native of India which appreciates warm conditions. Propagation is by short stem cuttings at any time during the growing season. Often stems will produce roots at their leaf joints and these pieces of growth can be detached and started as fresh plants.

Ludwigia mulertii As with most *Ludwigias*, this is essentially a swamp plant, but one which is equally at home when grown totally submerged. It has handsome lanceolate leaves of bronzy-green with crimson-purple undersides. Propagation is by stem cuttings during the growing season.

Marsilea quadrifolia Foil Plant, Water Clover. Although technically ferns, these strange aquatics look rather like four-leaved clovers. Their other common name alludes to the manner in which their foliage unfurls beneath the water, their hirsute foliage retaining air at its surface which gives the new leaves the appearance of being made of tin foil. *Marsilea* is a creeping plant which will quickly colonise the floor of a tub or pool, and it is this creeping rootstock that can be chopped into little pieces for propagation purposes.

Myriophyllum hippuroides The tropical milfoils are equally as valuable and attractive as their hardy counterparts. This species in particular has an important role to play in the cultivation of tender aquatics. Apart from its value as an oxygenating plant, and a competitor for water-discolouring algae, its bright green feather foliage is excellent for the deposition of spawn.

M. scabratum Every bit as good as the foregoing, this species has reddish-bronze foliage and occasional spikes of small purple flowers. Cuttings of both species should be taken regularly to ensure vigorous growth.

Riccia fluitans Crystalwort. This is a free-floating oxygenating plant which forms thick mats of starry foliage just beneath the surface of the water. A marvellous spawning plant that can be readily increased by division and redistribution.

Sagittaria lorata This plant belongs to the family that gives us that attractive native marginal plant, the arrowhead. Although not looking much like its hardy cousin, it does produce tiny turions or winter buds in exactly the same way. It has dense underwater foliage with the appearance of a spring onion in bold crowded clumps. These are over-shadowed during mid-summer by floating arrow-shaped or oval leaves amongst which tiny white flowers are produced. *Sagittaria subulata* is very similar but much smaller and with more grassy foliage. Both increase freely and advance across the floor of the pool or tub. Some of these advancing growths can be lifted and separated as individuals for propagation purposes.

Vallisnaria spiralis Tapegrass. This broad tape-like but grassy foliage plant with tiny white flowers is probably the best known tender submerged oxygenating plant of all. A frequent inhabitant of both coldwater and tropical aquaria it is equally useful for tub or sink culture. The shorter growing form 'Torta' has stout foliage which twists in a corkscrew-like fashion. Propagation is by separation and redistribution of the plantlets which cluster together.

CHAPTER 8

Fish for the Pool

Ornamental fish should not be introduced into a newly established pool until a month or so after planting, as they invariably root about amongst the plants, disturbing them and retarding their growth. When planting has been done in containers it is sometimes possible to introduce a few small fish at the same time, but it is not really advisable. Stocking with fish follows a similar formula to that advocated for planting to maintain a balance, for fish too have a considerable bearing upon the clarity and sweetness of the water. The initial stocking rate is all important, for although the maximum recommended is 6 in (15 cm) of length of fish to every square foot (0.093 sq m) of surface area of the water, a much lower rate of 2 in (5 cm) to the square foot is much more satisfactory. At this stocking level the fish will have an opportunity to grow, which they would be unlikely to do at the maximum rate and secondly, where breeding is envisaged, even on a modest scale, a maximum stocking rate would lead to casualties, especially amongst young fry. The calculation of the length of fish in the formula is based upon the total length nose to tail. Thus a total length of 3 ft (90 cm) may equally well be composed of three fish at 1 ft (30 cm) each or six fish of 6 in (15 cm) each. The surface area figure is based upon the total surface area of the pool excluding that occupied by the marginal shelves.

All the ornamental coldwater fish which are described here live happily together, with the exception of the catfish. Even young fishes, once they are past the fry stage, will mix quite happily with all sizes and both sexes of the varieties discussed. Fish of all kinds grow in accordance with their surroundings; thus a goldfish that has been confined to a bowl for a number of years will remain small, yet once introduced to a pool will grow quickly and attain sizeable proportions.

Ornamental
Fish for the
Garden Pool

Fish for the Pool

Bitterling (*Rhodeus sericeus amarus*) Most people regard this as an aquarium fish because of its small size and strange breeding habits, which can be more readily observed under aquarium conditions. However, it is a lively and desirable little fish for the pool, somewhat like a tiny carp, but with a lustrous metallic sheen. Neither male nor female grows more than 3 in (7.5 cm) long, the male being particularly attractive with a body coloration of intense blue and mauve which lasts throughout the breeding season. The female is a little more sombre, but during late spring can be readily identified by her long ovipositor, often equal to the length of the fish itself, which she uses to deposit her eggs in the mantle cavity of a living mussel — invariably the painter's mussel, *Unio pictorum*. Two or three are laid at a time, after which the male ejects his milt and the sperms are carried into the mussel through its inhalant siphon to fertilise the eggs. Incubation lasts about three weeks, the tiny fry only leaving their host when capable of leading an independent life.

Bronze Carp. This is a collective name used by the aquatics trade for any bronze-coloured carp-like fish, but usually refers to uncoloured goldfish. Bronze carp are cheap and useful fish for stocking large expanses of water, but cannot be unreservedly recommended for the small pool, particularly when goldfish breeding is envisaged as both forms will obviously interbreed and the dominant bronze colour will be prevalent in the progeny.

Common Carp (*Cyprinus carpio*) The common carp is a fairly dull, yet playful fish which is useful in the large pool, but not particularly valuable for the smaller water garden. It is usually a silvery or bronze colour, with a chubby, meaty body, narrow tapering head and four pendant barbels. Apart from its lack of bright colour, it is a great stirrer of the pond, nosing and probing in the plant containers for aquatic insect larvae and disturbing the compost. Indeed, this applies to most of the carp family, but can be more readily tolerated when the fish is visually appealing.

The Chinese red carp or Higoi is one such variation. A salmon or orange-pink fish of handsome proportions with a slightly more depressed head and typical pendant barbels. Of similar appearance, but bronze coloration, the scale carp is another form that often makes an appearance. Further variations with different proportions of visible scaling are the mirror carp, leather carp and band carp. All these are available from garden centres from time to time, but, although looking attractive in a tank or aquarium, are not so appealing when in the amber waters of the garden pool.

Crucian Carp (*Carassius carassius*) A similar looking fish to the common carp, but without the pendant barbels and depressed head of that species. A deep-bodied fish with a rich chocolate and bronze coloration, lightening to gold or greenish-yellow on the belly. Again a fish that does not show up too well in the pool compared with the brightly coloured goldfish varieties.

Dace (*Leuciscus leuciscus*) Although the dace can seldom be accommodated satisfactorily in a small pool owing to its large oxygen requirement, it is an attractive character for the medium or large-sized pool. The dace, like the orfe, is a surface feeding fish and does much to control the insect population. It is a handsome fellow of a steely-grey colour with a large head and long cylindrical body. Commercial stocks of dace are not plentiful, most of those offered for sale being of native origin, so one should always regard their purchase with caution. Indeed, any wild fish or fish suspected of having been caught in a river should not be introduced into the garden pool without having been quarantined for at least two months, preferably more. All rivers have diseases which the local fish are resistant to or live with, but once transferred to the relatively sterile conditions of the garden pool, cause havoc amongst the unprotected inhabitants.

Goldfish (*Carassius auratus auratus*) The goldfish is probably the best known of all coldwater fish. A sprightly, hardy fellow that is available in colours that range from red, pink and orange through yellow to white. Apart from obvious differences in colour, the most striking divergence from the true goldfish is the transparent scaled variety which is known popularly as the shubunkin. In this, the body appears to be smooth and scaleless and in a wide range of colour combinations. Reds, yellows and shades of blue and violet intermingle and are often and variously splashed and stained with crimson or black. Some of the specific colours and colour combinations have been selected and bred so that now there are strains which have been given names. Two of the best known of these are the Cambridge Blue Shubunkin and the Bristol Blue Shubunkin. The former has an even base colour of powder-blue overlaid with violet and occasional patches of ochre, while the Bristol Blue is characterised by a blue base which is heavily overlaid with violet and mauve and liberally splashed with crimson.

99

Figure 8.1:
Common Goldfish

Figure 8.2:
Shubunkin

Figure 8.3: Comet

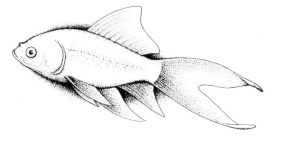

One of the most attractive variations of both the common goldfish and the shubunkin is the comet-tailed form, sleek looking fish with a long, flowing tail often as long as the body, and giving the appearance of a comet. In the blue strains of shubunkin these are exceptional and comparable with anything the tropical aquarist can offer. Fantails and moors are further variations, but in these the bodies are short, rounded and dumpy and sport handsome tripartite tails. The fantails are typically goldfish in every other respect and the moors have bulbous telescopic eyes as well. Typical goldfish-like fantails are referred to as red or red and white fantails and the shubunkin types as calico fantails. The moors are sub-divided as well, the shubunkin types being known as calico moors, goldfish kinds as red telescopes and the variety with a velvety black body as the black moor.

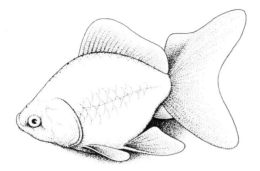

Figure 8.4: Fantail

There are also twin-tailed goldfish of the same general aspect as fantails, and these are known as veiltails. They are slow swimmers which by virtue of their excessive finnage are compelled to swim in a rather humorous wiggling fashion. Developments from these are the oranda, which has a strange strawberry-like excrescence on its head, and the lionhead which has a similar, but exaggerated, growth which calls to mind a lion's mane. Apart from this it is like a veiltail goldfish, but devoid of a dorsal fin. However the most amazing diversion of all is the celestial, a fairly typical goldfish with a flattened head that bears two upward pointing, staring eyes.

All goldfish and shubunkins are hardy in their natural forms, but most of the fancy kinds are short-lived if not given a measure of protection during the winter. This need merely be sufficient depth in which to overwinter, for while the common kinds will tolerate being frozen in the ice for a day or two, their fancy cousins will not. A minimum depth at one point in the pool of 18 in (45 cm) usually ensures an ice free area for the more susceptible fish to retire to.

Gudgeon (*Gobio gobio*) Most pool owners regard this quaint little character as a scavenging fish, for once introduced to a pool it is rarely seen, preferring to inhabit the murky depths and root about in the mulm. Gudgeon are strange looking fish, having elongated, somewhat cylindrical bodies, long

Figure 8.5: Oranda

Figure 8.6:
Lionhead

Figure 8.7: Celestial

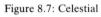

tails and large heads which sport pendant barbels. Beloved
of small boys, these may be regarded as curios rather than
striking inhabitants of the garden pool.

Koi Carp. Of complex parentage the Koi or Nishiki-koi are
amongst the most startling members of the carp family. It is
their fine livery that is the attraction, iridescent colours and
shiny mirror scales which give some of the bronze and
yellow selections a metallic appearance. Colours vary from
red, orange, yellow and pink through the glowing metallic
bronzes and steely-blues to grey, violet and white. Some of
these strains or selections have been named by the Japanese
and occasionally one will be able to purchase a fish by its
name. Thus we have at present amongst the better named
kinds 'Shiro-ogen', pure white, 'Sanke' which is white with
red and black, and 'Ki-ogen', a lovely yellow selection. In

shape they are like all the other carp varieties, being strong and meaty with a well formed head and often short pendant barbels. At the present time the Koi has a large and enthusiastic following and there are Koi societies in many parts of the country.

Minnow (*Phoxinus phoxinus*) Our native minnow is a great asset to the garden pool and, although preferring shallow water and a stony bed adapts well to life in captivity, particularly if there is a fountain or waterfall beneath which he can play. Minnows are by their very nature gregarious fish and are better introduced to the pool in quantity. Although small fish, they bring a pool alive with their flitting and darting movements which give flashes of steely-grey. In the breeding season the males turn very dark, almost black, and have a reddish belly and conspicuous crimson markings at the corners of the mouth. For the remainder of the season they revert to the more drab silvery-green of their partners.

Orfe (*Idus idus*) This is a handsome fish for the medium-sized and larger pool. As with other shoaling fish it should be introduced in quantity. As it is very energetic the water must be well oxygenated. Orfe love nothing better than dancing in the spray of a fountain or leaping about beneath a waterfall. The ordinary species is known as the silver orfe, its salmon-pink variation, the golden orfe. Even in perfect conditions the orfe seldom breeds successfully in Britain, which is something of a mystery as it is bred commercially in large numbers in Germany.

Figure 8.8: Golden Orfe

Roach (*Rutilus rutilus*) Although not strictly speaking a pond fish, the roach adapts readily to pond conditions, particularly where there is some movement in the water. The roach is similar in appearance to the dace, of a steely-grey colour, but with bright red irises to the eyes. Unlike the dace it appears to be more solitary and occupies the middle area of the pool rather than the surface.

Rudd (*Scardinius erythrophthalmus*) While the common rudd is seldom offered to the pool owner, its lovely silver and golden variations are frequently available. Like the orfe they tend to keep close to the surface of the water and are generally observed swimming around in groups. The silver rudd has something of a metallic look about it and conspicuous red fins, while the golden variety is of a coppery hue rather than a solid yellow or orange colour. Where there is ample space and plenty of underwater plant growth, rudd will breed quite freely.

Figure 8.9:
Common Rudd

Scavenging Fish for the Garden Pool

Most pool owners believe that their pool will not function satisfactorily without scavenging fish. This is a misconception brought about by the belief that the scavengers will act as living vacuum cleaners and suck up and devour all manner of debris, mud and stones, or else completely clear the pool of slime and algae. If one considers that all the fish commonly advocated as scavengers are predominantly carnivorous in their feeding habits, then one can appreciate that this is a fallacy. What scavengers actually do is clear up uneaten goldfish food which falls to the bottom of the pool and thereby prevent it from decomposing and fouling the water. Therefore if one has a well balanced pool and does not regularly feed the goldfish, the scavenger is largely unnecessary, although most pool owners feel more contented if one is present.

Catfish. In the coldwater fish trade the collective name catfish refers to three species: the horned pout (*Ameiurus nebu-*

losus), brown bullhead (*Ictalyrus nebulosus*) and the German wels or waller (*Silurus glanis*). All three species are similar in appearance, having long barbels or whiskers and similar habits. These habits by and large are undesirable, and any pool owner contemplating introducing any of this trio into the pool should be aware of their mode of life. While it is true that they will scavenge and devour uneaten fish food from the pool floor and prey upon aquatic insect life, once they have attained adult proportions they generally turn their attention from worms and insects to young fry and the tails of fancy goldfish. Indeed, those of varieties like fantails, moors and comets are frequently shredded beyond recognition. Therefore the use of the species referred to loosely as catfish can only be considered when other large fish are involved and breeding not contemplated.

Green Tench (*Tinca tinca*) The green tench is the most usual scavenging fish, a sleek character with short broad olive-green body and narrow tapering head. Like other scavenging fish, once introduced to the pool it is seldom seen, preferring to lurk amongst the mulm on the bottom in its quest for gnat larvae and similar delicacies. Although tench will seldom breed in a small garden pool, if you want a pair they are readily distinguishable once 6 in (15 cm) or so long. The male has a much larger pelvic fin, it being strong and distinctive and often reaching as far as the anal orifice, while that of the female is very small and weak. Apart from the ordinary tench there is a golden variety which looks excellent in the coldwater aquarium, but as it naturally lurks on the bottom it is of little decorative value in the outdoor pool.

Figure 8.10: Green Tench

Fish for Tubs or the Indoor Pool

It is a great temptation to step over the thin line that divides the aquarist from the pool owner when recommending fish to inhabit the indoor pool or tubs with tropical waterlilies, for almost all those that are popularly recommended for the tropical aquarium are sufficiently adaptable to be able to establish themselves successfully under these conditions. However, there are two kinds of fish which are on the borderline of hardiness in Britain and these, together with fancy selections of the common goldfish, are unquestionably the most satisfactory fish to consider.

Bass and Sunfish. The pool owner will generally have difficulty in identifying the various varieties of bass or sunfish that are sold commercially as these may belong to any one of three genera: *Elassoma*, *Mesogonistius* or *Enneacanthos*. However, this is of little account, as all are on the borderline of hardiness. All are noted for marvellous iridescent colours; blues, yellows, bronze and green in a multitude of patterns and combinations, heightened with spots, splashes and bands of darker colours. They are all carnivorous and mostly pugnacious so only specimens of similar size should be mixed together. While they feed satisfactorily on ordinary flaked goldfish food, the occasional earthworm or portion of daphnia is appreciated, particularly when they are confined to a tub. While it is possible to persuade bass to breed in a confined space, this is a lively business and the growing medium and plants get disturbed in the process.

Medeka or Rice Fish (*Oryzias latipes*) These are splendid little fellows that will occasionally winter outside, but are best provided with a degree of protection. They are small fish, seldom more than 1½ in (3.75 cm) long, and in commercial stocks a rich orange-yellow or golden colour, a considerable departure from the drab olive-green of the wild species. Medeka breed readily; indeed I have persuaded them to reproduce in a two gallon bucket, so the fish fancier has every prospect of success. The main requirement is a temperature around 70°F (21°C), and then they will breed at any season of the year. The female carries her ova around in a cluster attached to a narrow thread and after fertilisation she brushes them off onto the foliage of submerged oxygenating plants. Medeka love a feast of live daphnia, but are quite content with a staple diet of flaked tropical fish food.

Fish for the Pool

The selection of a well balanced mixture of healthy fish is essential if the pool is to be a success and the emphasis throughout should be upon health and quality. Never be persuaded that a particular fish is a bargain just because it is cheap. There are seldom any bargains to be had when purchasing livestock and fish are no exception. One might even say that the selection of healthy well proportioned fish is more important than selecting strong vigorous aquatic plants, for one can often transform a weakly plant into a healthy one by a little care and feeding, but a sickly or malformed fish usually remains so for life. This is why I am against the purchase of pond fish by mail order. Not that I doubt the integrity of the majority of companies selling fish in this manner, it is just that one does not have a clear idea of the health of the fish when they left the vendor's premises, neither is there any control over the colour selection that is received. A visit to the local garden centre or pet shop is infinitely better, for then it is possible to select particular individuals and get an overall impression of the health of the stock being offered.

Most dealers in coldwater fish keep them in large aquariums of fibreglass tanks or pools that are devoid of any plant material and supplied with air from a pump. This may seem a very unhealthy manner in which to keep them, but in fact it is the most satisfactory both from the customer's point of view and that of the retailer. The purchaser has a good clear view of what he is being offered and the retailer can keep his tanks more scrupulously clean when they are devoid of plant life, which incidentally would interefere with the simple process of netting one's purchases. The only time to be suspicious is when one tank is connected to another, or when fresh water is being constantly introduced and the surplus drains away via an overflow. In the first case there is a likelihood of disease being spread rapidly from one tank to another, and in the other, the constant introduction of fresh turbulent tap water leads invariably to the breakdown or reduction of body slime on the fish, which in turn leaves it wide open to disease once introduced to the relatively impure water of the garden pool. The idea behind adding fresh water constantly to a tank of fish is to prevent the build up of the troublesome whitespot disease (see page 140) by washing the free-swimming stage of its life-cycle away. The most reliable purchases can be made from a static tank of fish in which perhaps an air pump bubbles, and where the water has that nice matured amber look about it. Common goldfish and shubunkins come from Italy or the southern United States, golden orfe from Germany and fancy goldfish and both Higoi and Koi carp from Japan, Singapore or Hong Kong. This does not mean that they will be vulnerable in colder climates, because all adapt readily. The reason that they usually come from more equitable climes is that they breed more profusely and colour much sooner, and this generally makes them more economical to produce. However, it is the wise pool owner who enquires of the vendor how long the fish he intends purchasing have been in the country, for they are often rushed from airport to wholesaler to garden centre in two or three days and could be swimming in your garden pond a week after leaving Singapore. Clearly this is not a good idea, so if you doubt the vendor's word when he tells you that his fish have been in this country for several weeks, look at the colours, particularly of the goldfish. Those that are bright red, orange or yellow are recent imports, for once removed from a stock pond into a selling tank they lose their brightness. This takes three or four weeks, bright red fish fading to salmon-pink and vivid yellows changing to ochre. These can be purchased with confidence, as they have been effectively quarantined for almost everything except white spot disease, and after reintroduction to a pool will regain their vivid hues. This colour fading seems to be applicable to all coldwater pondfish except the fancy carp which seem to retain their strong colours irrespective of their environment. Green tench should be of a greyish colour. Never purchase a dark coloured tench from a batch of lighter coloured ones as it will almost certainly be dead the following morning. For some reason tench in their death throes turn almost black and swim close to the surface of the water with an uneasy gait. Catfish perform in the same way and if you must have one, then go for a specimen of a lighter hue.

Figure 8.11:
Features of a fish

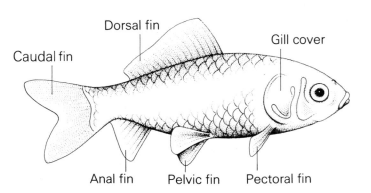

Dorsal fin

Gill cover

Caudal fin

Anal fin   Pelvic fin   Pectoral fin

The best indication as to whether a fish is in good health is the condition of its fins. A stout upright dorsal fin and well expanded pelvic fins indicate a fish that is healthy and this can be confirmed if the eyes are clear and bright as well. An obvious consideration when choosing fish would be their liveliness, and while a lively fish is likely to be a healthy fish, it could equally well be a very hungry fish. It is an old dealer's trick to keep fish hungry so that they will swim and dart about in search of food and therefore appear livelier than they would be ordinarily and the added bonus is a reduction in the fouling of the tank. With small fish it is important to see that there are no damaged or missing scales as exposed tissue is very susceptible to fungal infection. The same applies to larger specimens, although it is not quite so critical, and the likelihood of finding a large fish that has no scales missing is very small. The problem is that economic pressures dictate that live fish be transported in quantity in large polythene bags with a little water in the bottom and blown up with oxygen, thus leaving the fish vulnerable to knocks and damage. If an otherwise healthy fish has a few scales missing the simplest precaution to take is to dip it in one of the proprietary fungus cures based upon methylene blue or malachite green. In fact it is a wise precaution to treat all newly purchased fish, giving them a dousing with a solution of either as a disease precaution before introducing them to the pond. It is very important that the manufacturer's instructions regarding the dilution rate are carefully followed.

Sometimes white spots, rather like tiny raised pin heads, will be seen on the bodies of the fish. These are invariably associated with white spot disease, which although curable, takes a long time to overcome. Indeed, if a retailer's premises is infected with white spot disease it will take a number of weeks for him to put things right, and while it may only be evident in a single tank it is likely to have spread throughout his stock for it is easily distributed with a net. It is important, though, that this disease is not confused with the nuptial turbucles which appear in profusion on the gill cover, head and sometimes front or pectoral fins of normal healthy male fish. While looking like the pustules of white spot they are very localised around the head area. The fins will have an upright stance and the fish a bright eye, which is a complete contrast to a white spot infected specimen in which the eye will look misty and the dorsal fin will seem to have collapsed.

There are no other serious points to consider, for the ideal colour shape and conformity of the fish are a matter of personal whim. Specific species do have their own short-comings and a number are afflicted by maladies that are specific to them. One of the most serious is the condition in carp known as 'Big Head'. This manifests itself as one would imagine in an enlarged and distorted head, but is also characterised by a pinched body which reinforces the belief that this is some tubercular infection. No matter what its cause, when selecting carp it is essential to avoid any that appear to have larger heads than normal, and while consider-ing physical defects one must not overlook the strange crooked backbone deformity that is not infrequently seen in tench.

Irrespective of whether fish are purchased by mail order or from the local pet shop or garden centre, all are now packed in heavy gauge polythene bags which are usually blown up with oxygen. Fish travel quite happily this way under normal circumstances, but it is advisable to ensure that large specimens are packed individually. If the weather is hot or thundery resist the temptation to purchase fish like golden orfe that have a high oxygen requirement, for even in small sizes they will succumb on the way home.

Freshly purchased fish should be introduced to the pool gradually. If the bag is blown up with oxygen allow it to float on the surface of the pool for a short time so that the temperature of the water inside becomes equalised with that in the pool, and then gently pour the fish out. With fish that have travelled overnight by rail the same procedure should be adopted, but a meal shortly after their arrival would be greatly appreciated as the fish will have been starved for a couple of days before despatch to ensure that they do not foul the water in the bag excessively while in transit. New arrivals are often nervous for a few days, lurking amongst the submerged plants and hiding amongst the lily foliage, but confidence soon develops and after a week or ten days they are usually as active and visual as their comrades.

Feeding Fish

The general care and well being of coldwater fish and their breeding in the garden pool is covered in the next chapter, and while feeding also comes under the broad heading of general care, it is probably more appropriately discussed here, for it is immediately that fish are introduced to a newly established pool that feeding is required and if necessary a long-term strategy decided upon. In the established pool feeding the fish is largely unnecessary as there are always sufficient aquatic insects and their larvae around to satisfy the most voracious appetites. Notwithstanding this, most pool owners enjoy feeding their fish and get quite a thrill when the fish swim to the surface at the sound of a footfall or in response to a shadow falling across the water. Regular feeding at the same place in the pool encourages such a performance. However, feeding fish can be likened in many ways to feeding plants, for not all species have the same requirements and overfeeding can be both wasteful, and in a small pool dangerous, as any uneaten food decomposes and pollutes the water.

Balanced fish foods are available in three different forms: the conventional or crumb food, usually in a multitude of colours from white and ochre to red and vivid yellow, and often the by-product of biscuit manufacture; the flaked types of food which are also multicoloured, but take the form of thin tissues of flake rather like a much refined breakfast cereal; and finally the floating pellet varieties which are brownish in colour and look not unlike the green pellets that commercial rabbit breeders feed to their charges. All have their advocates and all their drawbacks. Both pelleted and flaked foods float for a considerable length of time and allow one more readily to observe the fish feeding. On windy days the flakes are not such a good idea as they are carried on the breeze and end up out of the reach of the fish in the tangle of marginal plants at the poolside. It does not matter too much which food is used, or even if a combination of diet is provided, for fish change readily from one form of food to another and will continue to prosper providing that their nutritional requirements are satisfied.

Fish appreciate variety in their diet and specific kinds of foods are available to provide this. Dried flies, daphnia, shredded shrimp and ants' eggs are freely available, although the nutritional value of the latter once dried and packaged is open to question. Fish generally prefer the real thing, and while not advocating a search for fresh ants' eggs, if one happens to stumble across a nest in the garden it is worth setting up a trap in which to gather the eggs. A small box like a match box has a tiny hole cut out of it to provide an entrance. The box is then inverted and placed close by the ant hill which should have been disturbed to ensure that the eggs will be transported from the main nursery to a safe depository. On spying the inverted box with the tiny hole the ants believe that this is a safe refuge and start to move the eggs into it. Once the removal is complete, the box can be lifted and the eggs removed. Live foods are much appreciated by all fish. Gnat larvae, mosquito larvae and daphnia or water fleas are occasionally found in water butts and similar receptacles and can be netted with a fine mesh net and fed to the fish. Daphnia can be cultured to provide a constant food supply throughout the summer. A tub of soft water is set up with an inch (2.5 cm) or so of soil in the bottom and allowed to settle. A net full of live daphnia is added and proliferation will be so rapid that a small harvest of succulent insects can be garnered each week.

The feeding of conventional packeted food, once the pool is established, depends upon the weather and the time of year as to the amount and frequency given. Throughout the summer months the equivalent of a pinch of food for each fish on alternate days would be adequate. Another good guide is the speed at which the fish clear up the food. Any that remains after twenty minutes should be netted off and the rate of feeding reduced until a happy balance is achieved.

Other Livestock for the Garden Pool

Snails and Mussels

Apart from the fish there are other livestock that can be introduced to the pool to assist in maintaining a natural balance. Snails of certain species are useful in that they devour rotting vegetation and algae, especially the soft filamentous species that cling to the pool walls, planting baskets and the foliage of submerged plants. They are also good indicators of the condition of the water in the pool. In water with a high pH value their shells are smooth and lustrous, whereas in acid water they become brittle and badly pitted. Mussels also assist in ridding the pool of algae, for they act as filters sucking in water and then blowing it out again, but retaining the suspended algae.

Great Pond Snail (*Limnaea stagnalis*) Although frequently for sale as garden pond snails, this species has a voracious appetite for aquatic plants and should never be introduced, for while it does feed to some extent upon algae it much prefers the succulent floating pads of the waterlilies which it reduces to unsightly holey scraps of vegetation. Apart from this it is an intermediary host for a fish disease which passes in a circle from the seagull, via the snail to the fish. When established in the pool it can be controlled by floating lettuce leaves or an old cabbage stalk on the water overnight. In the morning all the pond snails in the vicinity will be clinging to it and can then be removed and destroyed. *Limnaea stagnalis* is easily recognised as it has a

tall, spiralled and pointed shell an inch (2.5 cm) or more
high and a fleshy greyish-cream body. It lays its myriad eggs
in long cylinders of jelly which can often be detected on the
undersides of waterlily leaves and the foliage of submerged
aquatic plants. Removal of these at an early stage helps in
the control of the species. Two other kinds of *Limnaea* are
sometimes sold for garden pools and, while not so
destructive as their larger cousin, cannot be unreservedly
recommended. They are diminutive characters, the Ear
Pondsnail (*Limnaea auricularia*) having a less twisted shell
and enlarged aperture, and the Wandering Pondsnail
(*Limnaea peregrina*) sporting a very smooth shell, which is
much less twisted.

Ramshorn Snail (*Planorbis corneus*) This is the only species of
snail that can be unreservedly recommended for the garden
pool. A handsome creature with a somewhat flattened shell
which the creature carries in an upright position on its back.
The shell may be likened to a small catherine wheel and is
not likely to be confused with any other species encountered. There are red-fleshed *P. corneus* var. *rubra* and
white-fleshed *P. corneus* var. *albus* varieties in addition to
the common species which is black. All three are perfectly
hardy, despite the fact that the coloured forms are often
used in tropical aquaria. If the various colours are
introduced to a pool for the sake of variety, black will
ultimately predominate, for black is the dominant colour
and during the course of breeding will swamp the other
variations. Snails are hermaphrodite, but are unable to, or
rarely, fertilise themselves. In addition one mating by a snail
is sufficient for several batches of eggs, so the colour of the
progeny for some time will be dependent upon the colour of
the male element at that all important early mating. Eggs of
the ramshorn snail are laid on submerged plant life in flat
sticky pads of jelly about ½ in (1.25 cm) in diameter. They
are much sought after by fish, which regard them as a
delicacy, and so overpopulation is a rare occurrence.

Painter's Mussel (*Unio pictorum*) Not the most useful or
spectacular of the freshwater mussels, but an interesting
character as it is often the host or surrogate mother of the
progeny of the common bitterling (see page 98). A
diminutive fellow, it has a yellowish-green shell conspicuously marked with brown growth rings.

Swan Mussel (*Anadonta cygnea*) This is the species that is
most frequently available and undoubtedly the most useful
for the garden pool. However, it is not advisable to

introduce them to very small bodies of water for they enjoy cool conditions and a liberal accumulation of mulm on the pool floor through which to crawl or bury themselves. Neglect in this regard will result in rapid death and extremely unpleasant decomposition in the water, which in turn will entail the emptying of the pool and render a thorough cleaning essential. It is not an unattractive species, frequently attaining a length of 4 or 5 in (10-12.5 cm), with an oval dull, brownish-green shell which contains a white fleshy body.

Frogs, Toads and Newts

Rarely does a pool owner introduce any of these creatures to his pool, but invariably one or other species makes its home in the water garden and its presence often causes some alarm. There is nothing to be concerned about because all exist happily with fish and cause no undue damage or disturbance to plant life. For some species like the great crested newt it is one of the last refuges available, for farm ponds are quickly disappearing, together with its natural habitat. Some fish keepers express misgivings at the presence of a frog, for it is known that occasionally a lone male frog will attach itself to a fish during the breeding season, clasping it around the gills from behind in typical breeding stance and causing considerable damage. The pleasure that frogs give the average pool owner far outweigh the occasional problems they cause.

Common Frog (*Rana temporaria temporaria*) This popular creature is too well known to need description, but the other two species now naturalised in Britain and native to the USA, the edible frog (*R. esculenta*) and the marsh frog (*R. ridibunda ridibunda*) are perhaps not so familiar, even though the former has been with us for something like 150 years. This is of a typical muddy green colour, but with a distinctive pale stripe down its back, while the adult marsh frog is almost twice the size of the common species. All breed during spring and early summer, the common kind being the first to be seen. Both males and females enter the water and remain there for several days, the male embracing the female from behind and hugging her tightly. When amplexus, as this process is known, has finished the female deposits her spawn into the water, whereupon the male ejects his sperm into the mass. Once fertilisation has been completed, the jelly-like masses with tiny black spots are slowly transformed into tiny tadpoles. These at first feed upon algae, but as they metamorphose their tastes change and they become exclusively carnivorous. Around this time their tails begin to disappear and tiny legs develop. After three or four months they resemble tiny versions of their parents and in three or four years are themselves breeding freely.

Common Toad (*Bufo bufo bufo*) Toads live a similar life to frogs and breed in a very similar manner. They are not generally as appealing in the garden pool for they have a tough brownish, warty skin, an ungainly walk and are mainly nocturnal. They are amongst the greatest friends that a gardener can have for they feed almost exclusively on slugs, snails and other garden pests.

Common Newt (*Triturus vulgaris vulgaris*) These small, lizard-like creatures spend part of their life-cycle in the pool, the remainder in its surroundings, eating insects and by and large making themselves useful. An added bonus for the patient observer are their springtime courtship dances in the pool. During these the male contorts his body and flicks his tail violently for several minutes before depositing a spermatophore which is taken up by the female into her cloaca. The sperms from this then make their way along the oviduct to fertilise the eggs, which are then individually released and wrapped collectively in the leaf of a submerged plant several days later. Breeding continues well into summer, but by the end of July the parents have left the water to spend the remainder of the year on land. The common species is of a brownish or olive colour, but the male displays a wavy crest along his back and a bright orange patch on his belly. The palmate newt, *T. helveticus helveticus*, is of a similar habit and appearance, except that both male and female are much smaller than the common kind and the male has a much lower, straighter crest and webbed toes.

Great Crested Newt (*Triturus cristatus cristatus*) This is usually a much more persistent aquatic species than its smaller cousins, extending its stay in the water until well past the breeding season. It is a handsome fellow 6 in (15 cm) or more long with a long tapering crest and black body with contrasting bright yellow belly. The garden pool is un-questionably the last refuge of this disappearing British native which now enjoys the full protection of the 1981 Wildlife and Countryside Act, so it is a creature that should be encouraged.

Fish for the Pool

Pond Tortoises and Terrapins

There are at least five different species of these lovable lumbering reptiles which can be accommodated in the garden pool, but only two are widely offered by the aquatics trade in Great Britain. Both will live happily in the pool and should not unduly affect the balance or way of life of the other inhabitants. That is not to say that they should be introduced in quantity, but a pair would be a most attractive addition to the average garden pool and apart from consuming an occasional small or ailing fish would be of little consequence. They do not require fencing in for they never stray far from water, unless of course there is a sizeable lake next door, and being carnivorous will not chew garden plants in the same way as the ordinary domestic tortoise. In the USA it is illegal to sell or own tortoises or terrapins privately, so these species will, of course, not be available to the amateur.

European Pond Tortoise (*Emys orbicularis*) A most attractive kind with a black or deep brown 'shell' or carapace liberally sprinkled with yellow spots. Its black head and clawed toes are splashed with yellow while its long whip-like tail is black. When full grown it can be 8 in (20 cm) long and will often try to breed, with variable success. As a former native of Britain it should be possible to raise young here, but I have never come across anyone who has done so without resorting to some artificial means of incubation. When an egg is noticed remove it from the pool margin or bog garden and place it in a box of moist sand at a temperature of 70°F (21°C), possibly in an airing cupboard or somewhere similar. The eggs of the pond tortoise are soft shelled and if fertile will hatch after several weeks incubation. Following this the young tortoise can be placed in a heated aquarium at a temperature of 65°F (18°C), with provision made for him to rest on dry land if necessary. At this early stage a diet of minced meat or chopped worms is the most suitable. A closely related species, the American Pond Tortoise (*E. blandingii*), although not so colourful, is exceedingly hardy and well worth acquiring if the opportunity arises.

Spanish Terrapin (*Clemmys leprosa*) An altogether more reserved character, but one which can provide endless pleasure, swimming just beneath the surface of the water and popping his head up periodically like a periscope. The carapace can vary in colour from light olive-green to almost black, but is more likely to be the former. The legs and head

116

are mostly green but often striped and splashed with orange or yellow. Both this and the pond tortoise can be fed on canned dog or cat food and over a period of time become quite docile and are seldom aggressive towards fish or other pool inhabitants.

CHAPTER 9

Looking After a Water Garden

Maintaining a water garden is little differernt from any other feature of the garden, in so far as regular care and tidiness make for a healthy environment, and care and attention to detail bring their just rewards. It is because a water garden is such an alien feature to most gardeners that they are understandably perturbed, especially when caring for the fish. This is particularly apparent when preparing the pool for winter.

The Pool During Winter

It is a good idea to prepare fish for their long winter vigil by feeding them with high protein foods like dried flies, daphnia and ants' eggs during September and October. As soon as the weather turns cold the fish will cease to be active and feeding should be stopped and not considered again until the spring when they are seen darting about the pool once more. All common pond fish are capable of surviving during the winter months without feeding, as their body processes slow down in much the same manner as a tree or shrub which loses its leaves and becomes dormant. Neither are they too concerned about the cold, unless it becomes excessive.

It is ice rather than low temperatures which present the greatest hazard for the fishkeeper, for not only can it create great pressure upon the pool and crack the most proficiently laid concrete, but it traps toxic gases. These gases are formed all the year round and emanate from decomposing vegetation on the pool floor. Under normal circumstances they escape harmlessly into the air, but once a layer of ice has formed they eventually fill the narrow air space between the water surface and the ice and suffocate the fish. The only way to alleviate this problem is to ensure a continuous ice-free area. When a pump is used in the pool and removed for the winter months, the electrical point can be used to connect a pool heater. This consists of a heated brass rod with a polystyrene float and is perfectly safe to use, keeping an area of water free of ice in the severest weather.

Alternatively a hole may be made in the ice by placing a pan of boiling water on the surface and allowing it to melt through. Although this is a time-consuming method of releasing noxious gases, it does ensure that the fish are not subjected to the shattering shock waves which accompany a well-meaning person trying to break the ice with a pick or similar heavy instrument. To help prevent the ice from exerting pressure on a concrete pool and causing it to fracture, it is useful to float a sizeable piece of wood or a child's rubber ball on the water, so that the ice will exert pressure against an object which is capable of expanding and contracting.

There are no serious problems with the plants during the winter months. Waterlilies can be permitted to die down of their own accord, but any yellow leaves with soft crumbling edges or black spreading blotches should be regarded with suspicion, for they may be suffering from waterlily leaf spot and it would be prudent to remove them. Some gardeners express concern over their waterlilies during the winter months but, providing that they are covered by at least 9 in (22.5 cm) of water, there is usually no problem. Pygmy waterlilies, when growing in a shallow pool, can have the water drained off and will survive quite happily with a generous covering of straw or old leaves. A piece of board or a Dutch light frame placed over this will prevent the pool from filling with winter snow and rain. Once the fear of severe frost has passed the pool can be filled again and the plants started into growth.

Floating plants disappear for the winter months, forming turions or winter buds which fall to the bottom of the pool, to reappear the following spring when the water has started to warm up once more. During the autumn, before these buds disappear, it is a good idea to collect a few and place them in a large jam jar of pool water with a handful of mud on the bottom. These can be kept in a cool light place until the spring when they can be encouraged into growth by raising the water temperature. This ensures early growth and the plants can be put out on the open pool before water-discolouring green algae become a serious problem.

Algae

Algae is to a certain extent a problem for every pool owner, even if it is just for those two or three weeks in late spring when the water has warmed up, yet the higher plants are not in active growth and capable of providing sufficient competi-

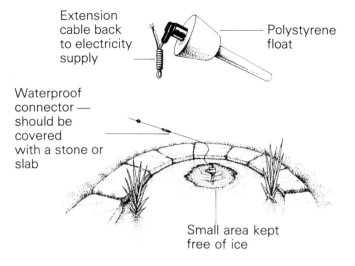

Figure 9.1: Example of a pool heater

Extension cable back to electricity supply

Polystyrene float

Waterproof connector — should be covered with a stone or slab

Small area kept free of ice

tion. Aquatic algae occurs in many forms, but these can be divided primarily into free-floating and filamentous. The free-floating kinds comprise in excess of four hundred species which swarm in great masses and give water the 'pea soup' effect. The filamentous kinds on the other hand appear as free-floating silkweed or spirogyra which can be dragged from the pool by the handful, or else in thick mats known as blanket or flannel weed. Other species like the mermaid's hair cling to plant and baskets and often coat the walls of the pool as well.

There are no magical cures for the various algal problems and the best permanent solution is based upon the theory of natural balance outlined earlier (see page 54); the higher plants providing competition for mineral salts and creating shade beneath. The chemical controls which are outlined here are at the very best only temporary solutions, but can be very useful in the early life of a pool when the higher plants are attempting to become established. Elimination of water-discolouring algae at this stage allows more light to enter the water and aids establishment of submerged oxygenating plants.

Free-floating algae can be controlled relatively easily using an algaecide based upon potassium permanganate, but must be treated on a dull day when the water is not too warm, or else the pool will turn a thick cloudy yellow and have to be emptied. On no account should potassium permanganate crystals be used on their own, as the margin of error is very small when fish and other livestock are involved and even some of the higher plants will succumb to an excessive dose.

Filamentous algae can be controlled with proprietary algaecides like the widely used Algymicin PLL, but after treatment all dead algae must be removed to prevent deoxygenation of the water. Of course it is possible to control algae with straight chemicals, but it is unwise to do so unless it is from a position of knowledge. The indiscriminate use of chemicals can be disastrous, and it is the accurate measuring of them for use in small volumes of water that creates the greatest difficulty. Copper sulphate can be used safely on a regular basis when applied in small quantities. In order to clear all algal growth and not affect the plants a concentration of 0.033 ppm must be used. Higher plants can stand considerably greater concentrations, but the fish will become asphyxiated by the copper sulphate combining with their body mucus. Care must also be taken over the relative hardness of the water as this has a marked effect upon its performance, the copper sulphate uniting with the carbonate of the calcium carbonate to form an insoluble precipitate of copper carbonate. Water temperature is also vital, for this may have an effect upon the reaction. In warmer water the unstable calcium bicarbonate normally found in tap water leaves a higher concentration of calcium carbonate, thereby reducing the effect of the copper sulphate.

Sometimes formalin is recommended as an algaecide, but it should be treated with caution, for while it will rid a pool of algae it can also have strange effects upon other plants. Several varieties of waterlily break into rapid growth with their leaf stalks extending by several feet and the deep water aquatic *Nymphoides peltata* is completely destroyed at very small concentrations. In the past sodium arsenite has been used as an algaecide and is occasionally recommended, but its use is no longer permitted by amateur gardeners, despite the fact that it is very effective.

The Neglected Pool

Algae is only one problem of the gardener who acquires a neglected pool, a situation facing many people when they move house. There is scarcely anything more disheartening than an overgrown water garden, for not only is it unsightly and smelly, but it is not easily removed, so even the most uninterested person will make an attempt to come to terms with it.

A lot will depend upon the time of year as to how the pool will appear. One that has seemingly few plants and crystal clear water during the winter may become a tangled mass of foliage obscuring thick green water during the summer. Of course the water may disappear entirely for the summer months owing to a leak which cannot be easily detected during the winter because of the higher water table of the surrounding ground. So it is during the summer that a neglected water garden should be appraised, for not only is it then seen at its worst, but if any plants are going to be salvaged, they have a much better chance of survival and re-establishment at that time.

When the pool is full of water, then it must be drained away before a start can be made. Older pools sometimes have a removable plug for this purpose, but after years of neglect they are often difficult to locate. It is most likely therefore that siphoning or baling will have to be resorted to. When part of the surrounding ground is lower than the pool there is no problem. A length of garden hosepipe is merely filled with water and while one end is held in the pool with the thumb over it, the other is smartly removed to the lower area. Providing that the action is quick and the thumb removed immediately the end of the hosepipe is lower than the surface of the pool, the pull of gravity will ensure that the flow continues.

When a bucket has to be resorted to, special care should be taken to ensure that fish and other livestock are not thrown out. Fish usually gravitate to the accumulated mulm and debris on the pool floor, those like catfish and tench remaining until the very last and thrashing around in a minimal amount of mud and debris. It is useful to have several buckets full of clean water standing in a shady corner in the garage or somewhere similar, so that any refugees can be quickly accommodated.

A decision must be taken about which livestock are going to be reintroduced to the pool and which are to be discarded. Catfish, as was mentioned earlier, are pugnacious and when these are discovered they should be given to someone with an aquarium where they can live peacefully on their own. Although while young they are useful in that they devour all manner of insect pests, once of sizeable proportions they turn their attention to snails and small or fancy fish. All the other varieties of pool fish are compatible and live happily together, although it is wise to inspect them for signs of fungus and white spot disease (see page 140) and take appropriate remedial action. Even when the fish appear clean and healthy it is a sensible precaution to treat them all with a fungus cure based upon malachite green before putting them back in the pool. Small brown or silvery fish that look like tiny carp are generally uncoloured goldfish. Some attain their adult colours when quite young, but others take several years to turn gold, while a number will remain bronze. How many are reintroduced to the pool will depend upon the current level of stocking and the additions that it is envisaged making.

Fish that are rescued from a derelict pool need temporary accommodation in a cool place such as the garage. The containers in which the fish are kept need not be very deep, but should have as much surface area as possible and a clump or two of submerged plants can be introduced to provide a little green matter in their diet. The fish will of course need regular feeding with an ordinary dried food, but will benefit if occasional live fare can be provided. The snails should be kept separately from the fish, preferably in a large bucket with a wad of filamentous algae, for if introduced into spartan conditions with the fish they will be dragged out of their shells and eaten. The ramshorn snails are the ones to retain as these feed almost exclusively on algae. They are easily recognised by their catherine wheel-like shells which they carry in an upright fashion on their backs. Pointed snails, especially those of the whelk family, should be discarded for, as we discovered earlier, these are very partial to waterlilies and other succulent aquatics and can be as troublesome in the pool as garden snails are on the allotment.

Badly neglected pools have little in the way of plant life, except the two or three stronger growing species that have swamped everything else. These are usually much less desirable characters like the bur reed, reedmace or soft rush. Waterlilies are almost always worth rescuing, certainly if they have mottled foliage, for there is no cultivar with blotched or mottled leaves that is not garden worthy. However, it is wise to regard large green-leafed kinds with suspicion, for although they look lovely and healthy they are likely to be one of the forms of our native white waterlily, *Nymphaea alba*, which requires a farm pond or lake in which to do itself justice. Waterlilies with horizontal rootstocks are likely to have been derived from *N. tuberosa*, *N. odorata* or one of their forms and these are all most desirable, while tiny rounded-leafed kinds with correspondingly small rootstocks should be treasured as these will almost certainly be *pygmaea* varieties or possibly of the *laydekeri* group.

There are seldom any marginal plants that are worth rescuing, but anything with variegated foliage and obvious garden worthy subjects like irises should receive attention. All species and varieties of sedges, rushes and reeds should be consigned to the compost heap, for it is extremely unlikely that anything that is so vigorous will be desirable. Floating plants are not likely to be discovered at all, except in high summer, for they spend a considerable part of their life on the pool floor, appearing on the surface of the water during late May and early June, but disappearing by the middle of September. The various species of duckweed often survive and proliferate, but these should be treated with caution as they are invasive and can create problems when the pool is being re-established. Few submerged oxygenating plants are able to survive in a neglected or overgrown pool, but where growth is evident short cuttings can be taken and made into bunches, each fastened with a strip of lead or wire. These cuttings will then produce fresh vigorous underwater growth. Before removing submerged plants find some alternative accommodation for them as they can only remain out of water for a couple of hours without spoiling, and with some species less than that.

Once everything that is any good has been removed, the remaining mud and debris should be taken away to another part of the garden, where it can be allowed to dry out and incorporated with the general garden soil. Never be tempted to use healthy looking mud for propagating or repotting aquatics as it will doubtless contain the seeds of pernicious water weeds, loathsome characters like the fish leech, as well as diseases like waterlily root rot. None of these causes any trouble amongst ordinary garden plants, so the rich organic debris and mulm can be used freely in the garden.

Few pools that are constructed with a pool liner will survive after prolonged neglect and drastic cleaning, although with the rubber variety there may be a case for tackling minor damage. Polythene and PVC pool liners are best removed entirely, even if they look in reasonable condition, and replaced. Vacuum-formed plastic and fibreglass pools are usually all right and just need scrubbing before fresh plants are introduced. Concrete on the other hand may have suffered, although it is difficult to assess leakage problems unless damage is fairly extensive. Whatever the pool is made of, it must be carefully surveyed before replanting and refilling with water.

Under most circumstances pool liners will need to be replaced. Only where there are minor splits or damage of rubber kinds are repairs worth considering. These are treated in much the same way as a cycle inner tube with a puncture and the repair kit is almost identical to that of a cycle repair outfit. It is not practicable to repair polythene or PVC liners, even though repair kits of various kinds are sometimes offered, for the repair will at best be only temporary. Polythene liners only have a useful life of three or four years and the PVC kinds cannot be relied upon after ten, so careful consideration should be given to the kind of liner installed, for neither of these makes a permanent feature.

It is rare for fibreglass or vacuum-formed plastic pools to suffer damage, even when the pool has been neglected. It is impossible to repair the plastic kind satisfactorily, but a fibreglass pool that has a crack or severely crazed surface can be patched with the standard motor vehicle repair kit. Repairs can seldom be carried out *in situ*, so the pool should be removed and thoroughly cleaned. Fibreglass patching is not difficult to achieve successfully providing that the kit manufacturer's instructions are carried out on a clean pool and in a warm dry atmosphere.

Even when a pre-formed pool is not in need of repair it will often require realignment. A pool that is not level can cause problems with flooding at the low end and always looks unsightly when one portion is exposed. It is difficult to realign a pool without taking it out of the ground, but this having been done it can be rebedded in the manner described earlier (see page 16).

A pool constructed of concrete is the most permanent. Properly laid concrete seldom cracks or flakes and is good for many years. Sadly few pools are satisfactorily made and within a short space of time create problems for their owners. This is particularly evident when the pool has been neglected. One of the most frequent problems is severe flaking of the surface of the concrete owing to frost or a bad or inconsistent mixture of cement and aggregate. Under these circumstances little can be done except to line the shell with a pool liner. The surface is generally too abrasive for polythene or PVC liners, but rubber ones can often be installed successfully and are reasonably permanent.

Fractures in a concrete pool can usually be dealt with, although one should be aware that however good the repair, such a point is a place of weakness and may be a source of recurring trouble. With straightforward cracks the fracture line should be chipped out with a cold chisel in a 'V' shape. This must be roughed up to allow the concrete of the repair to key successfully to it. A conventional mix of one part cement, two parts sand and four parts gravel measured out with a bucket or shovel is used in cases where the concrete can be allowed to dry out naturally. When this is impossible a quick setting cement can be substituted. The ingredients are mixed in their dry state until of a uniform greyish colour and, if desired, a waterproofing compound can be added at this stage. Water is then added and the concrete mixed until the agglomeration is of a wet stiff consistency.

The old concrete must be thoroughly soaked with water before the repair is made. Patching is carried out with a plasterer's trowel and smoothed level with the adjacent surfaces. It takes several days to set properly, and even though the repair may look to be perfectly adequate, there is always the prospect of continued seepage. A wise precaution is to obtain a neutralising agent and paint this over the freshly concreted area. As was mentioned earlier, the free lime in new concrete is injurious to fish, so this is a sensible precaution to take. The most popular kinds of neutralising agent seal the concrete by internal glazing. To add further security to the repair, a pond sealant should be painted over the new concrete and adjacent area of the old.

Replanting of re-lined and pre-formed pools can take place immediately they are ready. Concrete pools on the other hand require a drying out period to allow repairs to dry so that they can be sealed properly. Once this is done, and providing that it is the season for planting aquatics, re-establishment can commence.

Propagating a Few Plants

The propagation of waterlilies has already been described (see page 27) and mention has been made of the best means of increasing individual plants along with their descriptions. However, a discussion in general terms is appropriate, as the means of propagation used varies slightly from the conventional. Taking division, for example, this consists of dividing an individual plant into several portions each with a strong shoot and of sufficient size to be capable of an independent existence. In many kinds, such as *Typha* and *Scirpus*, which produce a creeping rootstock, this involves removing a length of root with a terminal shoot attached and planting it separately. Obviously when such plants are divided it is usual to cut them down, but be careful not to replant with the cut ends of the stems below the surface of the water. Being hollow these fill with water and the plants are effectively drowned. With clump-forming plants like *Iris* and *Caltha* the individual divisions are more like small plants and are pulled away from the main plant by hand or with a small fork in the same way as one would deal with an herbaceous plant.

A number of plants that are readily divisible are also easily increased from stem cuttings and usually produce better plants when propagated this way. Amongst these are the water mint and brooklime. Short cuttings about 3 in (7.5 cm) long are removed from the parent plant during spring when vigorous growth is being made. If these are inserted in a tray or pot of sandy loam they will root within a fortnight. Both the plants noted are better replaced each year from vigorous young cuttings. So are submerged oxygenating plants when they need moving or renewing. Never try to move an established clump of submerged plants. Always take short cuttings and bunch them with a strip of lead or piece of wire and then insert them in their final position in a heavy compost. As long as the lead or wire is buried they will root quickly and soon form strong plants.

Winter buds or turions provide another means of propagation for a diversity of aquatic plants, from the submerged oxygenating hornwort to the robust marginal plants known variously as arrowheads or duck potatoes. The gardener need do little to aid this means of propagation except redistribute the turions according to the form which they take. Some marginal plants produce similar organs which are designed rather as a means of reproduction than as storage organs. These include the lovely flowering rush which has clusters of tiny bulbils around its fleshy rootstock. If these are gathered during spring, just as their fine foliage is emerging, and planted out in trays of mud they will rapidly form independent plants that can be planted in their permanent quarters the same summer.

Seed as one might expect is the most useful method of propagating a number of important aquatic plants, but only those that are species, rather than garden hybrids or cultivars, are likely to come true. Indeed, some of the garden forms do not set seed, a particularly well-known example being the double flowered form of the common marsh marigold. With all aquatic subjects it is advisable to sow seed immediately it ripens and for some plants like the water hawthorn it should not be allowed to leave the water before sowing. Others like the pickerel germinate more freely when sown green, while the Arum family — which embraces the golden club, skunk cabbages and bog arum — should be well ripened, but not allowed to dry out. The majority of aquatics will germinate in a wet heavy loam compost although those with floating foliage appreciate water over their crowns once through the soil. It is not advisable to submerge freshly sown seeds as they are often very light and float right out of the compost. To prevent algal growth on the surface of the compost it is advisable to provide a light covering of silver sand.

Breeding a Few Fish

There are few pool owners who are not delighted when they see some young fish swimming happily about in their pool. Not only is it rewarding to know that conditions are suitable for breeding, which in turn is a good indicator of a happy natural balance, but the excitement of counting the new arrivals and watching them change to their adult colours is a bonus, the like of which does not occur in other facets of horticulture. The beauty of it all is that one can treat fish breeding as seriously or casually as the fancy takes one, for providing the pool is in good condition the fish will do their stuff without the aid of the pool owner. It is only when something special is desired that man need interfere, and then only to help things along a bit.

All the fish that the pool owner is likely to have require the same kind of conditions if they are to breed satisfactorily and all reproduce in a similar manner except for the catfish and the bitterling (see page 98). The majority will belong to the *Cyrpinid* or carp family and many of these will be capable of interbreeding. But before attempting to start breeding fish seriously it is essential to fulfil at least some of their environmental requirements. Indeed, if fish breeding is a prime objective, then the pool should have a sizeable shallow area uncluttered by marginal plants, but thickly planted with submerged oxygenating subjects. This provides suitable conditions for the deposition of spawn and, if cleverly constructed, allows the periodical separation of the area from the main pool, thereby preventing the parents from preying on their young.

The breeding season in Britain extends from April until August, the fish being stimulated by the warmth and light intensity associated with spring and summer. The majority of goldfish are sexually mature in their second year, although adulthood is related more directly to size than age. Any goldfish 3 in (7.5 cm) or more in length should be capable of breeding. When purchasing suitable parents — and this is not a bad idea if one wants a reasonable balance of the sexes at the outset — choose fish with a good conformation, colouring and a bright eye, all characteristics that are desirable in their progeny. Matched pairs are commonly sold by aquatics dealers, and while they are obviously quite capable of breeding with each other, it does not follow that they will do so in the pool, for if there are other fish of the same species they may pair up with these. Generally like breed with like, but hybrids in the carp family are common and those of similar shape and constitution do interbreed. However, the fact that they are of the same family does not mean that fish as diverse as tench and mirror carp will unite.

Choosing a good pair of breeding fish from the retailer is not difficult if one knows the finer points to watch out for. Health is obviously a prime consideration and all the characteristics of a healthy fish described in Chapter 8 should be ascribed to those intended for breeding. From a purely breeding point of view, colour and conformation must be prime requirements and any scaling or other desirable feature also taken into account. Sexing fish in the spring is relatively easy. A female fish when viewed from above has an oval or elliptical body shape while that of a male is slim and pencil-like. The male is further enhanced by white pimple-like nuptial turbucles which are liberally scattered about the gill plates and head. Large females with distended bodies that look full of spawn should be avoided as having been kept in restricted surroundings may be suffering from spawn binding (see page 142).

Spawning takes place at varying intervals throughout the breeding season, their frequency being associated with water temperature rather than any other factor, although nobody is by any means certain. During spawning the male fish chases the female around the pool and amongst the submerged oxygenating plants, brushing and pushing furiously against her flanks. She then releases the spawn, trailing it in and amongst the stems and foliage of submerged plants. The male then releases his milt or sperm-bearing fluid amongst the eggs which then become fertilised. Once this has been observed, the area in which the spawn has been deposited should be separated from the adults, or else some of the submerged plants covered in spawn placed in an aquarium or large bucket. It is important that the water comes from the pool so that it is of the same temperature and composition. Tap water spoils the spawn, often causing it to grow fungus.

Natural spawning is usually satisfactory for most pool owners, but where specific unions between male and female fish are required an artificial method known as stripping has to be adopted. Although this can in theory be done at any time during the breeding period, June and July are the best months, for there will be females in the pool that have not spawned and will obviously be in a suitable state to do so. A chubby female with the desired characteristics should be carefully netted and examined. If the vent is distended and slightly reddened, then the fish will be in a suitable condition for stripping. This involves holding the fish in wet hands and applying gentle pressure to the sides of the belly, slowly progressing towards the vent and over a flat bottomed dish containing a little water. When done confidently and rhythmically the eggs will cascade into the dish and can be easily distributed by moving the fish backwards and forwards.

A suitable male must then be selected, great care being taken during netting not to induce premature emission of his milt by his jumping about in the net. Gently stroking the flanks should result in the emission of the milky-white milt which should be distributed as evenly as possible over the waiting spawn. Successful stripping can only be undertaken with firm and confident handling. Pinching and squeezing only damages the fish.

Fertilisation takes pace when the milt and eggs are in the dish, and will have been completed after twenty minutes or so. The spawn can then be gently rinsed with lukewarm water to reduce the incidence of fungal attacks. It is possible to hatch the eggs in the dish, but an aquarium is preferable. After three or four days the fry will be seen developing like tiny pins clinging to the submerged plants. After a couple of weeks they will become recognisable as fish, sometimes transparent, sometimes bronze, but eventually attaining their correct adult proportions and colours.

CHAPTER 10

Pests and Diseases

As with all features in the garden, the pool is subject to a wide variety of problems. Fortunately few of them need be the cause for any great anxiety, but control of even modest pest and disease problems amongst aquatic plants is difficult, for the slightest trace of insecticide or fungicide in the pool can lead to disaster with the fish and snail population. Fish need isolating when disease breaks out as it is so easy to transmit disease problems through the water: although much can be done to prevent disease becoming rife by the careful selection and quarantining of newly purchased fish before introduction to the main pool. Pests and diseases always make depressing reading, but forewarned is forearmed and the successful pool owner will familiarise himself with the problems that are likely to occur, so that at the first hint of trouble action can be taken.

Common Plant Pests

Beautiful China Mark Moth (*Nymphula nympheata*) We will not go into the life-cycle of this little moth, for it is almost identical to that of the next to be discussed — the brown China mark moth, one of the greatest insect pests to trouble the pool owner. All that is prescribed for this species applies equally to the less common beautiful China mark moth. The only difference is that the caterpillars of this burrow into the stems of aquatic plants in the early stages of their life and eventually hibernate there, later emerging to make leaf cases and ultimately their white, silky cocoons. The only control at present is hand picking.

Brown China Mark Moth (*Nymphula stagnata*) As mentioned earlier, this is a significant pest in the garden pool, cutting and shredding the foliage from aquatic plants and providing a shelter for itself prior to pupation by sticking down pieces of leaf in which it weaves a greyish silky cocoon. The damage to plants can be extensive, chewed and distorted leaves crumbling towards the edges and surrounded by

131

pieces of floating, decaying foliage. The eggs of these destructive caterpillars are laid during late summer in neat rows along the floating foliage of aquatic plants. Within a couple of weeks the tiny caterpillars emerge and burrow into the undersides of the succulent foliage and later make small oval cases out of these leaves. They continue to feed in this manner until the winter, hibernating for the winter period but reappearing in spring to continue their trail of destruction and weave the cocoons (described earlier) prior to pupation. Small infestations can be hand picked and all pieces of innocent looking floating leaf should be netted and discarded as they may have cocoons attached. When damage is widespread it is sensible to defoliate all aquatic plants with floating leaves and consign the debris to the bonfire. All the plant species likely to be affected will rapidly regenerate healthy growth.

Caddis Flies. There are many species of caddis fly, all of which have larvae which feed to some extent upon the foliage of aquatic plants. Many are totally aquatic at their larval stage and swim around with little shelters made from sticks, sand shells and pieces of plant surrounding them. Of the species commonly encountered, *Halesus radiatus* and *Limnephilus marmoratus* are most likely to be troublesome. These visit the pool in the cool of the evening, depositing up to a hundred eggs at a time in a mass of jelly which swells up immediately it touches the water. Often it will be hooked around submerged foliage in a long cylindrical string, or attached to a marginal plant so that it can trail in the water. The larvae hatch out after ten days or so, immediately starting to spin their silken cases and collecting debris and plant material with which to construct their shelters. At this time they feed voraciously upon aquatic plants, devouring leaves, stems, flowers or roots with equal indifference. They eventually pupate in the pool or amongst the rushes at the water's edge, emerging as dull coloured moth-like insects with greyish or brown wings. Chemical control is impossible, as the pests hide themselves in their protective shelters, but an adequate stock of fish will keep the population under control.

False Leaf-mining Midge (*Cricotopus ornatus*) Not a serious pest of aquatic plants, but an irritating little creature that has larvae which eat a narrow tracery of lines over the surface of the foliage of floating-leafed aquatics. The eaten areas start to decay and large areas of leaf become detached and decompose. Forcible spraying of the foliage with a strong jet of clear water is the most effective control.

Waterlily Aphis (*Rhopalosiphum nymphaea*) A widespread and troublesome pest of waterlilies and all succulent aquatic plants which breeds at a prodigious rate in warm humid weather. It attacks leaves and flowers with impunity, having the same effect upon aquatic plants that black bean aphis have upon broad beans. Eggs from the late summer brood of adults are laid on the boughs of plum and cherry trees during early autumn for overwintering. These hatch the following spring and the winged female adults fly to the plants. Here they reproduce asexually, giving birth to live wingless females which continue to reproduce every few days. As autumn approaches once again, winged males and females are produced which unite sexually and then fly to the plum or cherry trees to deposit their eggs. During the summer the only control is forcibly to spray the foliage with water and hope that the fish will clear up the pests before they have the opportunity to crawl back onto the foliage. Standard proprietary insecticides can be used if there are no fish or other desirable creatures in the pool. Much can be done to reduce the overwintering population by spraying all the plum and cherry trees in the garden with a DNOC tar oil wash.

Waterlily Beetle (*Galerucella nymphaea*) This is a very unpleasant and difficult pest to deal with, but fortunately only of local and occasional occurrence. Waterlily leaves become stripped of their epidermal layer by the shiny black larvae and then begin to rot. The tiny dark brown beetles hibernate during the winter in poolside vegetation and migrate to the waterlilies during early June. Here they deposit eggs in clusters on the leaf surfaces and a week or so later hatch out into curious little black larvae with yellow bellies. These feed on the waterlily 'pads' until pupation occurs, either on the foliage or surrounding aquatic plants. Under suitable conditions as many as four broods can be produced in a season. Spraying forcibly with a jet of clear water to dislodge the pests is the only remedy, although the removal of the tops of marginal plants during early autumn will do much to prevent the adults from hiding in the vicinity of the pond and hopefully dissuade them from launching such a vigorous attack the next season. Where there are no fish present, spraying them with malathion is an effective cure.

**Common
Plant
Diseases**

Waterlily Leaf Spot (*Ovularia nymphaerum*) This appears as dark patches on the foliage, which rots through and causes the eventual disintegration of the leaves. It is always prevalent in damp humid weather and as soon as noticed, affected leaves should be removed and burnt. Another kind of leaf spot, attributed to various of the *Cercosporae* species, is not quite as common, but equally destructive. The foliage becomes brown and dry at the edges, eventually crumbling and wasting away. Removal and destruction of all diseased leaves is the only effective cure, although a weak solution of Bordeaux mixture sprayed over the foliage is often recommended for checking its spread, but I would regard this as a last resort and use it with great caution.

Waterlily Root Rot. The root rot common to waterlilies is caused by one of the *Phytophthora* species, a relative of that familiar garden disease, potato blight. Waterlilies with dark or mottled foliage, especially yellow cultivars, appear to be the most susceptible. The leaf and flower stems become soft and blackened and the roots take on a gelatinous appearance and are foul-smelling. Affected plants must be removed immediately and destroyed before they infect their neighbours. When special waterlilies are in danger of becoming infected and it is possible to remove the fish, impregnating the water with copper sulphate provides protection. The crystals should be tied in a muslin bag, attached to a long stick and dragged through the water until completely dissolved.

**Common
Pests of Fish**

Anchor Worm (*Lernaea carassii*) Popularly referred to as the anchor worm, this horrible little pest is not technically a worm, but a crustacean which preys on members of the carp family. It is a destructive little character with a slender tube-like body about $1/4$ in (6.2 mm) long with a barbed head which embeds itself into the flesh of its host causing unsightly lesions and tumour-like growths. They often become covered in an algal growth and then look particularly sinister. Control can only be effected by capturing the host fish, holding it in a wet cloth and then touching the parasites with a brush dipped in a solution of potassium permanganate or ordinary household paraffin. This kills the parasites which can then be withdrawn with tweezers and the open wound dressed with an antiseptic disinfectant solution such as Dettol.

Dragonfly. All the species of dragonfly native to Britain and

134

the USA have naiad or developing stages which are predatory upon fish. As naiads can vary in their period of development within species and between species from one to five years, then one can readily appreciate that the problem is an almost permanent and certainly long-term one. Dragonfly naiads are unpleasant looking creatures resembling small scorpions and varying in colour from green and brown to grey. All their formative life is spent in the water clinging to submerged and partially submerged aquatic plant life just awaiting suitable prey to pass by. When a suitable candidate is seen, the naiad shoots forward a 'mask' from beneath its chin. This 'mask' is like a pair of jaws with strong hooks which grip the unfortunate victim and then retract and bring the prey back to the naiad's mouth. Although dragonfly naiads of native species are really quite small and can seldom eat a fish in one go, they are capable of causing very unpleasant injuries and should be removed from the pool whenever noticed.

Fish Louse. Fish lice are parasitic crustaceans of the genus *Argulus*, and cling to the bodies and gill plates of all kinds of pool fish. Each species or family of fish seems to have a specific louse, those infesting goldfish being quite different from those preying upon catfish. All look superficially alike, with a flattened end and shell-like carapace with a small abdomen projecting, and feeler-like appendages at the anterior end that are used for attachment to the host. Males and females look identical, but it is only the females that are parasitic. These can be easily dislodged if the affected fish is held in a wet net and the parasites are dabbed with a drop of paraffin from a child's paint brush. As the tissue beneath may have been damaged the fish should be dipped in a solution of malachite green as recommended for the treatment of fungal diseases, before reintroduction to the pool.

Great Diving Beetle (*Dytiscus marginalis*) There are several native species of diving beetle which prey upon fish, but it is the adults and larvae of the great diving beetle that present the greatest problem. Up to 2 in (5 cm) long, the adult beetle is a handsome fellow with a hard, oval-shaped, chitinous body of dark brown with a distinctive golden border. The larvae are of similar appearance to dragonfly naiads, but seldom more than $1\frac{1}{2}$ in (3.75 cm) long. Being splendid aviators, the adults can spread quickly from pond to pond and all one can do is to net them out whenever seen before they have an opportunity to reproduce.

Great Silver Beetle (*Hydrous pictus*) The adult beetle which is so familiar in ponds and streams in the countryside in southern Britain causes no trouble at all when it makes its home in the water garden. It is the larvae that it sires that creates havoc, devouring small fish, tadpoles and feasting upon water snails at any opportunity. The larvae are seldom less than 2 in (5 cm) long, more or less sausage-shaped, of a dark brown colour, with three pairs of legs just behind the head which it uses to drag its ugly body along. Control is very difficult as the beetles can travel freely from one pond to another.

Hydra. Anyone who studied biology at school will know of these strange little creatures of octopus-like appearance which spend their lives attached to submerged plants, capturing prey by means of stinging tentacles which paralyse the victim that they have ensnared. Their usual diet consists of worms and water fleas, although severe infestations can decimate the fish fry population. *Hydra viridissima*, *H. oligactis* and *H. vulgaris* are the three native species which are likely to be encountered and all look similar to the naked eye, although there is a colour range which extends from brown to ochre and grey. Control is difficult as they are so very small. Handpicking is not practicable, for while they are visible to the naked eye, once the plant that they are clinging to is touched, the hydra virtually 'dissolve' into an indistinct gelatinous mass, only to reappear when the plant is reintroduced to the water. Only if they are being particularly troublesome is it worthwhile trying a chemical control, for this involves removing the fish and adding an ammonium salt to the water and then emptying and refilling the pool with fresh water.

Leeches. Traditionally leeches are abhorred by man, but none of our eleven or so native species could be said to strike terror in the hearts of anyone. All are harmful in varying degrees to both fish and snails, but it is only the fish leech, *Piscicola geometra*, which makes itself a nuisance. In common with other leeches it has numerous blind sacs within its body for storing blood which it sucks from its hapless victims. One gorging generally lasts for some time, and during this period it just lingers about harmlessly amongst the water plant digesting its meal. All our native leeches are hermaphrodite, sometimes mating in pairs, but self-fertilising as well. They generally attach their eggs to aquatic plants, although at least one of the minor species carries its eggs around with it. Control is difficult, but where there is a severe infestation a piece of raw meat suspended in the water from a length of string will attract considerable numbers which can be removed and destroyed. Fish with leeches attached should be held in a wet net or cloth, and a dab of salt administered to the tail of an assailant will cause it to detach itself.

Water Boatmen. There are two families of insect which are loosely referred to as water boatmen, but it is only those of the family *Notonectidae* that are harmful to life in the pool. They feed chiefly upon other aquatic insects, tadpoles and fish spawn, but are capable of inflicting nasty wounds upon large fish and killing small fish outright. The harmful water boatmen swim on their back, whereas the harmless kinds swim on their bellies. The commonest of the harmful species is *Notonecta glauca*, a small, roughly oval-shaped creature about ½ in (1.25 cm) long with a conspicuous triangular mark in the centre. Its legs appear like oars and propel the little creature through the water at great speed. Control is not easy and must be confined to regular netting and disposal.

Water Scorpion (*Nepa cinerea*) This is a vicious little fellow up to 1½ in (3.75 cm) long with a strong pair of front legs with which it grabs its prey, and a mouthpiece which it uses to pierce and suck its victim dry. Looking just as one would imagine a scorpion should look, it sits motionless amongst aquatic plants or on the floor of the pool just awaiting suitable prey to pass by. It breeds during the spring, depositing its large eggs amongst decomposing plant remains and blanket weed, so general pool hygiene deprives them of suitable places to breed and forms an important part of their control. Handpicking is possible when they can be seen.

Water Stick Insect (*Ranatra linearis*) This relative of the water scorpion has similar vicious habits. It is slightly larger than its cousin, with a very thin body and although perhaps not so frequently noticed, can cause trouble if not discouraged by pool hygiene.

Whirligig Beetle (*Orectochilus villosus*) Anyone who has ever sat beside a pool for any length of time will have seen these remarkable little, black, rounded beetles which deposit eggs on the roots and submerged foliage of aquatic plants. These hatch into small yellowish-white larvae, roughly cylindrical in shape, and with three pairs of legs and several pairs of feathery appendages. They feed predominantly upon other aquatic insect life, but also delight in attacking small fish. Control of the larvae seems impossible and while handpicking of the adults is tiresome it is the only effective means of keeping the population within bounds.

Common Diseases of Fish

Dropsy. The condition known variously as dropsy or scale protrusion is of bacterial origin. Afflicted fish become distended with their scales standing out from the body and their internal organs filled with fluid. This can be drawn off with a hypodermic needle, but as the organs become quickly filled again and the operation is tricky, it is only worth considering as a last resort when a valuable fish is involved. Commercially it is possible to overcome this disease with injections of antibiotics, but it is not a remedy open to the home gardener and an afflicted fish should be dispatched as quickly and humanely as possible (see page 143).

Fin Rot and Tail Rot. A number of bacterial infections have been blamed for this unpleasant condition, although the main culprit has yet to be isolated. A fairly common disorder, it usually manifests itself on the dorsal fin, spreading to others and reducing them quite quickly to a mere stub. The first sign of the disease is a whitish line along the outer margin of the fin which gradually advances downwards, leaving the outer margin badly frayed owing to disintegration of the soft tissue between the hard rays of the fins. If infection creeps as far as the flesh the fish will almost certainly die, but if an affected fish is noticed in time, the badly frayed tissue removed with a pair of sharp scissors and the fish placed in a fungus cure, the infection will be defeated and much of the lost tissue will regenerate.

Fungus. Every time a fish damages itself in any way it becomes open to attack from one of the fungal diseases. These are of the genera *Achyla* and *Saprolegnia* and apart from attacking living fish, can often be seen on fish spawn and uneaten goldfish food, which points to the value of scavenging fish and the importance of pool hygiene. When a large fish becomes infected with fungus it is a relatively simple matter to clear it up provided, of course, that the infection is not too severe. Conversely with fry and small fish it is almost impossible and any tiny fish that become infected should be humanely destroyed at an early stage. There are innumerable fungal cures available, mostly based upon malachite green or methylene blue, and these are used according to the manufacturers' instructions as dips into which diseased fish are immersed. A salt bath is often recommended, and while this can be beneficial, it is a slow and unreliable

138

method of treating this ailment. If salt must be used ensure that it is rock or sea salt, not iodised table salt. When the fish has been dipped in one of the more recent proprietary fungus cures, the cotton wool-like growth of the fungus should fall away. After the fish has been reintroduced to the pool keep an eye open for re-infection as the raw areas of tissue will still be vulnerable. An aid to fungus prevention is the use of a fish food containing the anti-fungal ingredient saprolegnil. While this cannot be claimed to be foolproof, it is believed to provide some measure of protection.

Gill Flukes. Once again the species of two genera are responsible for this distressing condition, the *Gyrodactylus* and the *Dactylogyrus*. They are minute, invisible to the naked eye but have a very noticeable effect upon their hosts, causing them to swim in a violent and irrational manner, banging against the walls of the pool and period-ically rushing to the surface of the water as if having a fit. The rate of breathing of an infected fish is greatly increased and the constant twitching of the fins is a further symptom of this malady. Various cures based upon mild disinfectants and formalin have been tried with varying success in the past, but as at least half the fish treated die in any event, it is kinder to despatch the poor creatures as soon as the trouble is noticed.

Red Pest. An uncommon, but very infectious bacterial disease in which affected fish become sluggish and rise to the surface. Rusty-red patches appear on the flanks and undersides, and sometimes on the fins as well. It is best to destroy the entire stock of fish unless very expensive specimens are involved. These can be kept in a tank of running water for several weeks, the constant flow of fresh water giving them hope of survival. However, as fresh tap water also destroys their body mucilage, it is questionable as to whether the danger of red pest can be eliminated before fungal infection takes over. A pool in which the fish have suffered from red pest should remain fishless for several months before restocking.

Slime and Skin Diseases. A number of single-celled organisms of the genera *Costia*, *Cyclochaete* and *Chilodonella* cause skin disorders and slime disease. Afflicted fish can often be seen swimming against the edge or bottom of the pool as if they are trying to scrape themselves and relieve an itch. They usually have folded fins and become covered in a bluish-white slimy deposit which would appear to be a combination of natural slime and parasites. Badly diseased fish must be destroyed, but those where it is believed there is hope can be bathed in a solution of acriflavine for two or three days.

Tail Rot *see* Fin Rot.

White Spot Disease or Ich (*Ichthyophthirius multifilis*) This is a widespread and destructive disease perpetrated by a member of the single-celled organisms known as *Protozoa*. It is much more prevalent in the warmer temperatures of aquaria, but is a not infrequent assailant of pool fish, having been introduced from freshly purchased stock that has spent a period of time in the more amenable surroundings of an aquarium. In the garden pool, where the water temperature is invariably lower, the life-cycle is slowed down and treatment can be effected before too much damage has been caused. It is a tiny organism, scarcely a millimetre across, but its presence for at least part of its life-cycle imbedded in the skin of a fish does have a considerable effect upon its host. Fish that have become badly infested look as if they have white measles, take on a pinched appearance, and swim in an ungainly manner. Severe attacks like this are difficult to cure and such fish are best destroyed at the outset. If a light sprinkling of spots is noticed on the tails or fins of a fish then this is generally curable, unless it is very tiny. Certainly young fry that show any infection at all should be destroyed.

White spot disease has several phases of development which must all be known to the pool owner if he is going to conquer it. In the initial stages the 'spores' or 'swarmers' are roughly pear-shaped and bore their way into the skin of a living fish. Here they feed upon their host until of an adult size and recognisable to us as white spots. The mature parasite leaves the fish through a hole in the skin and then becomes free-swimming, eventually encysting. Inside the cyst they divide into upwards of a thousand 'spores' which leave the cyst in search of a host. Obviously it is at the swarming stage that the disease can most effectively be controlled. The white spots which give the disease its common name are quite visible, but inaccessible until they rupture. At certain temperatures the free-swimming stage must find a host quicker than at others. The higher the temperature generally, the shorter the period that the swarmers have to locate a host, thus in higher temperature regimes this period may be as little as two days. Therefore if infected fish are placed in tanks at a relatively warm temperature the swarmers will be released more quickly, but if water is constantly flowing into the tanks these 'swarmers' will be regularly washed away. When a pool is known to be infected it may be several weeks at quite a warm water temperature before fresh fish can be safely introduced without fear of infection. Apart from attempting to wash away the free-swimming stage or starving the infection of a host, there are various chemical treatments that can be tried. Most are based upon an acriflavine solution, or else quinine salts like quinine sulphate or quinine hydrochloride and mixtures such as methylene blue and acriflavine. The fish are generally kept for a period in a solution of one of these chemicals, the free-swimming stage being killed as it emerges. The fish are pronounced fit when the white spots have disappeared completely.

Apart from the cures prescribed, there are other ways to fight the disease. The most useful is prevention, for white spot can be easily introduced on plants and fish purchased from the local garden centre. Fish should receive a quarantine period before being placed in an established pool, and if part of this treatment involves being treated with a white spot disease cure, then no problems will be encountered later on. Additional aquatic plants that might be added to a collection should also receive an inspection before planting and be dipped in a mild solution of potassium permanganate as a precaution against transmitting the disease.

Other Disorders

Cataract. Not a common ailment, but one which is certainly worth a mention. Affected fish develop a white film over the eye. This starts with the pupil and eventually envelops the whole eye. A mixture of one part by volume of iodine to nine parts glycerine dabbed on the eye with cotton wool twice a day will in some cases remove the film, although it may well return.

Chlorine Damage. It is inevitable that most pool owners have to fill their pools initially, or after cleaning out, directly from the tap. This water contains chlorine as a disinfectant for killing bacteria, but it can also be harmful to young fish and fry. In large volumes of water it takes some time to dissipate and occasionally fish will suffer from its toxicity. Damaged fish have very pale gills with edges that are bleached white and look decidedly unhappy. To prevent this occurring never introduce fish to a freshly filled pool, always leave the water standing for a week or so in order to allow the chlorine to evaporate.

Constipation. While the uninitiated are always amused to learn that fish can in fact become constipated, those who understand the problem a little more clearly are always troubled when symptoms of constipation are evident. The affected fish trails a stream of excrement from the vent interspersed with tiny bubbles. This is usually the result of an unbalanced diet and any starchy foods should be immediately withdrawn and the fish placed in an aquarium where it can be fed upon a diet of boiled chopped cabbage or spinach along with regular introductions of live food. If the condition persists the fish can be immersed in a solution of Epsom salts, but this is a last resort for if the change of diet has no effect within a few days it is more than likely that the fish will succumb.

Loss of Balance. This is a physiological disorder in which fish swim in a drunken manner or hang nose downwards in the water, or occasionally upside down. Sometimes constipation can bring about this condition, but it is more usually associated with a derangement of the swim bladder, the balancing mechanism of the fish. A number of dubious remedies are tried from time to time, including purging, altering the water temperature or the diet, but most are of little use. It is therefore better to put the fish out of their misery from the beginning, as they become increasingly distressed with each day that passes.

Spawn Binding. This disorder is more frequently encountered in the aquarium, but is not uncommon in the small garden pool. Under normal circumstances a female fish finds that it is possible to spawn when her body dictates. In the aquarium or small pool this is not always possible, especially when confined to an unpleasant crowded environment. In these circumstances the fish attempts to dissolve and reabsorb the eggs that were being developed for spawning. If this is unsuccessful, which is often the case when the female is undernourished, the eggs become hard and incapable of being expelled. They then decay within the fish and an accumulation of gas occurs which leads ultimately to the death of the fish. Stripping the fish as described on page 130 is occasionally successful and is well worth trying, although care must be taken to ensure that the internal organs are not damaged. Rather than trying to cure the condition it is preferable to try to prevent it from occurring. Fish with plenty of room and a varied diet seldom

142

suffer from spawn binding.

Tumours. Any hard or raised lump that appears on the body of a fish should be treated with suspicion. Sometimes it is the beginning of an anchor worm infestation, but where it quite clearly is not, then the unfortunate fish should be destroyed, for treating tumours on small fish is a hazardous and painful business. Some aquarists are prepared to use a razor to investigate and sometimes operate, but the success rate is very low.

Wasting. Some fish which look emaciated and have arched backs and pinched bodies are merely suffering from the passage of time, but more likely they have become infected with the virulent *Mycobacterium tuberculosis*, the instigator of fish tuberculosis. This cannot of course be contracted by humans, but it manifests itself on the fish in typical fashion, causing extensive wasting and eventual death with no prospect of relief or cure.

Deterring the Heron

The heron does not clearly fit into any of our categories, but he must be mentioned, for in some areas of Great Britain he is the biggest problem that the pool owner has got, although, in the USA, the problem does not exist to the same extent. Herons turn up unexpectedly and often at the crack of dawn, taking substantial fish and returning regularly to the pool until all have been devoured. Heron netting can be purchased to cover the entire pool, but this is unsightly and not very practicable as plants eventually grow through it and create all kinds of cultural difficulties. As herons always wade into the water to fish, they can be quite simply deterred by making a row of short canes about 6 in (15 cm) high around the perimeter of the pool. Black cotton or fishing line is then attached to these to make a low fence. When the heron next tries to wade into the pool his legs come into contact with something which he cannot see and this makes him nervous. Several attempts are usually made before the heron flies off to seek pastures new.

How to Destroy an Ailing Fish

In this chapter I have perhaps seemed to be a little too ready to condemn sickly fish to death, but not without good reason, for those that I have recommended to be despatched have invariably been beyond any rational person's belief in a cure, or else so distressed that it is the kindest way out. Making a recommendation is one thing, carrying it out is quite another, particularly if the fish in question has become something of a pet. I prefer to take the unhealthy fish in a dry cloth and dash it smartly against a hard surface such as a concrete floor. Death will be instantaneous.

Glossary

Amplexus   Amphibious mating act appertaining particularly to the toad and frog.

Anal   Situated near the anus.

Anther   The part of the stamen containing the pollen grain.

Axil   Angle between stem and leaf base.

Barbel   Small fleshy appendage.

Boss   A tight rounded cluster, usually alluding to stamens.

Bract   A leaf, in the axil of which a flower arises.

Bulbils   Tiny young bulb-like offsets.

Carapace   The shell of a tortoise, terrapin or beetle.

Caudal   Near the tail.

Cloaca   Reproductive and/or anal passage (when referring to amphibians).

Cordate   Heart-shaped.

Corm   An underground stem resembling a bulb.

Crustacean   One of the natural order *Crustacea* (crabs, prawns, etc.).

Cultivar   A named cultivated variety of plant.

Dentate   Toothed.

Dorsal   Near or belonging to the back.

Excrescence   An abnormal protruberance.

Flaccid   Soft or flabby.

Genes   The hereditary factor which is transmitted by each parent to offspring and which determines hereditary characteristics.

Genus   Group of species with common characteristics.

Glaucous   Sea-green, covered with a fine bloom.

Hermaphrodite   Bisexual.

Hirsute   Hairy.

Hybrid   Plant produced by the cross fertilisation of one species or variety with another.

Glossary

Inflorescence	The arrangement of a group of flowers.
Lamina	Leaf blade.
Lanceolate	Lance-shaped.
Milt	Sperm-bearing fluid of certain fishes.
Mulm	Detritus.
Mutant	A plant or animal which differs from its parents as a result of genetical change, usually without any external visible influence.
Naiad	Another name for a nymph, the aquatic larva of such insects as the dragonfly.
Octaploid	Having four times the basic chromosome number.
Obovate	Egg-shaped, but with a narrow end at the base.
Obovoid	Solidly obovate.
Orbicular	Rounded, with length and breadth about the same.
Ova	The female germ cells.
Ovaries	Pertaining to the ovaries which contain the ova.
Ovate	Egg-shaped.
Ovipositor	Egg-laying organ.
Ovoid	Egg-shaped.
Panicle	A loosely and irregularly branched flower cluster.
Pectoral	On or near the chest.
Peltate	Shield-shaped.
Petaloides	Brightly coloured and resembling petals.
Petals	The coloured leaf-like parts of flowers.
Petiole	Leaf stalk.
pH	The acid/alkaline status of a soil, etc. A neutral condition is taken as pH 7.0; all figures lower than this denoting degrees of acidity, those above alkalinity.
Pinnate	Divided into leaflets, coarsely feather-like.
Pistil	Female reproductive organ in a flowering plant.
Procumbent	Lying loosely along the surface of the ground.
Pubescent	Softly hairy.
Raceme	An inflorescence in which the flowers are produced on subsidiary branches from the main stem.
Rhizome	An underground stem lasting more than

	one season.
Rhomboidal	Roughly diamond-shaped.
Sagittate	Arrow-shaped.
Sepals	Usually green and leaf-like outer part of the flower.
Serrated	Toothed like a saw.
Serrulate	Toothed like a saw.
Sinus	Depression between two lobes or teeth.
Spadix	Fleshy spike-like flower head.
Spathe	Leaf-like sheath enveloping a spadix.
Species	The specific plant with a genus.
Spermatophore	Collection of sperm.
Spores	The reproductive cells of flowerless plants.
Stamen	Male reproductive organ in a flowering plant.
Stellate	Star-shaped.
Stigma	The top of a pistil of a flower.
Stolon	Shoot from a plant — a runner or sucker.
Translucent	Semi-transparent.
Trifoliate	Three-lobed leaves.
Tripartite	Divided into three parts.
Triquetrous	Having three acute angles.
Tuber	Swollen portion of stem or root of one year's duration.
Turbucle	Spherical or ovoid swelling.
Turion	Detachable winter buds.
Umbel	A flower cluster in which the stalks arise from a common centre on the main stem.
Viviparous	Live-bearing.
Whorl	A ring of leaves, flowers or petals.

Ready Reference Guide to Aquatic Plants

Plants under each category are arranged in the order in which they appear in the text.

Hardy
Waterlilies

The measurements that are referred to are the ideal depths at which each variety succeeds. They will all grow with some degree of success in slightly deeper or shallower depths.

White

Up to 1 ft (30 cm)	*Nymphaea odorata* var. *minor*
	Nymphaea pygmaea 'Alba'
	Nymphaea tetragona
Up to 1½ ft (45 cm)	*Nymphaea candida*
	Nymphaea caroliniana 'Nivea'
Up to 2 ft (60 cm)	*Nymphaea* 'Albatross'
	Nymphaea laydekeri 'Alba'
Up to 2½ ft (75 cm)	*Nymphaea* 'Hermine'
	Nymphaea 'Gonnere'
	Nymphaea 'Virginalis'
Up to 3 ft (90 cm)	*Nymphaea* 'Alaska'
	Nymphaea marliacea 'Albida'
Up to 4 ft (1 m 20 cm)	*Nymphaea odorata*
	Nymphaea tuberosa
	Nymphaea tuberosa 'Richardsonii'
Over 4 ft (1 m 20 cm)	*Nymphaea alba*
	Nymphaea 'Gladstoniana'

Yellow

Up to 1 ft (30 cm)	*Nymphaea pygmaea* 'Helvola'
	Nymphaea odorata 'Sulphurea'

Up to 2 ft (60 cm)	*Nymphaea odorata* 'Sulphurea Grandiflora'
Up to 2$\frac{1}{2}$ ft (75 cm)	*Nymphaea marliacea* 'Chromatella'
	Nymphaea 'Moorei'
Up to 3 ft (90 cm)	*Nymphaea* 'Sunrise'

Pink

Up to 1 ft (30 cm)	*Nymphaea tetragona* 'Johann Pring'
Up to 1$\frac{1}{2}$ ft (45 cm)	*Nymphaea caroliniana*
	Nymphaea caroliniana 'Perfecta'
	Nymphaea caroliniana 'Rosea'
Up to 2 ft (60 cm)	*Nymphaea odorata* 'William B. Shaw'
	Nymphaea 'Amabilis'
	Nymphaea 'Arethusa'
	Nymphaea 'Baroness Orczy'
	Nymphaea laydekeri 'Lilacea'
	Nymphaea 'Somptuosa'
Up to 2$\frac{1}{2}$ ft (75 cm)	*Nymphaea odorata* 'Eugene de Land'
	Nymphaea odorata 'Turicensis'
	Nymphaea 'Mrs Richmond'
	Nymphaea 'Newton'
	Nymphaea 'Pearl Of The Pool'
	Nymphaea 'Pink Sensation'
	Nymphaea 'Rene Gerard'
	Nymphaea 'Rose Arey'
Up to 3 ft (90 cm)	*Nymphaea odorata* 'Firecrest'
	Nymphaea 'Gloire de Temple sur Lot'
	Nymphaea 'Masaniello'
Up to 4 ft (1 m 20 cm)	*Nymphaea odorata* var. *rosea*
	Nymphaea tuberosa var. *rosea*
	Nymphaea marliacea 'Rosea'
Over 4 ft (1 m 20 cm)	*Nymphaea marliacea* 'Carnea'

Red

Up to 1 ft (30 cm)	*Nymphaea pygmaea* 'Rubra'
Up to 2 ft (60 cm)	*Nymphaea* 'Conqueror'
	Nymphaea 'Ellisiana'
	Nymphaea 'Fabiola'
	Nymphaea 'Froebeli'
	Nymphaea laydekeri 'Fulgens'
	Nymphaea laydekeri 'Purpurata'

Up to 2½ ft (75 cm)	*Nymphaea marliacea* 'Flammea'
	Nymphaea 'Meteor'
	Nymphaea 'William Falconer'
Up to 3 ft (90 cm)	*Nymphaea* 'Andreana'
	Nymphaea 'Gloriosa'
	Nymphaea 'James Brydon'
	Nymphaea 'Louise'
Up to 4 ft (1 m 20 cm)	*Nymphaea* 'Attraction'
	Nymphaea 'Charles de Meurville'
	Nymphaea 'Escarboucle'

Chameleon and Striped

Up to 1½ ft (45 cm)	*Nymphaea* 'Aurora'
	Nymphaea 'Comanche'
	Nymphaea 'Sioux'
Up to 2 ft (60 cm)	*Nymphaea* 'Graziella'
Up to 2½ ft (75 cm)	*Nymphaea* 'Indiana'
Up to 3 ft (90 cm)	*Nymphaea* 'Galatee'

Pondlilies

Up to 1½ ft (45 cm)	*Nuphar minimum*
Up to 2½ ft (75 cm)	*Nuphar japonica*
Up to 3 ft (90 cm)	*Nuphar rubrodisca*
Over 4 ft (1 m 20 cm)	*Nuphar advena*
	Nuphar lutea

Other Deep Water Aquatics

Up to 1½ ft (45 cm)	*Orontium aquaticum*
Up to 2½ ft (75 cm)	*Nymphoides peltata*
Up to 3 ft (90 cm)	*Aponogeton distachyus*

Marginal Plants

The majority of marginal plants grow in moist conditions of up to 6 in (15 cm) of water, although a few will tolerate slightly deeper conditions.

Name	Flower Colour	Flowering Period	Height	
Acorus calamus	Green	June-July	3 ft	(90 cm)
Acorus calamus 'Variegatus'	Green/ variegated foliage	June-July	2½ ft	(75 cm)
Acorus gramineus	Green	June-July	10 in	(25 cm)
Acorus gramineus 'Variegatus'	Green/ variegated foliage	June-July	10 in	(25 cm)

150

Appendix I

Name	Flower Colour	Flowering Period	Height	
Alisma parviflora	Pinkish white	June-Sept	1 ft 8 in-2½ ft	(50-75 cm)
Alisma plantago-aquatica	Pinkish white	June-Sept	3 ft 3 in	(1 m)
Alisma ranunculoides	Blush-pink	June-Sept	6 in-1 ft	(15-30 cm)
Butomus umbellatus	Pink	July-Sept	1 ft 8 in-2½ ft	(50-75 cm)
Calla palustris	White	April-June	8 in	(20 cm)
Caltha leptosepala	White	March-May	1 ft 4 in	(40 cm)
Caltha palustris	Yellow	March-May	1 ft	(30 cm)
Caltha palustris alba	White	March-May	1 ft	(30 cm)
Caltha polypetala	Yellow	March-May	3 ft	(90 cm)
Carex pendula	Brownish-green	May-July	2-3 ft	(60-90 cm)
Carex riparia	Brown	May-July	2-2½ ft	(60-75 cm)
Carex riparia 'Aurea'	Brown/golden foliage	May-July	2 ft	(60 cm)
Carex riparia 'Variegata'	Brown/variegated foliage	May-July	2 ft	(60 cm)
Cyperus longus	Greenish-brown	May-July	2-3 ft	(60-90 cm)
Cyperus vegetus	Reddish-mahogany	May-July	2 ft	(60 cm)
Damasonium alisma	White	June-Aug	1 ft	(30 cm)
Eriophorum angustifolium	White	May-July	1 ft-1 ft 4 in	(30-40 cm)
Eriophorum latifolium	White	May-July	1 ft-1 ft 4 in	(30-40 cm)
Glyceria aquatica 'Variegata'	Greenish-white/variegated foliage	June-July	2-3 ft	(60-90 cm)
Houttuynia cordata	Creamy-white	June-Aug	1 ft	(30 cm)
Hypericum elodes	Yellow	July-Sept	3-6 in	(8-15 cm)
Iris laevigata	Blue	June	2-3 ft	(60-90 cm)
Iris laevigata 'Alba'	White	June	2-3 ft	(60-90 cm)
Iris laevigata 'Colchesterii'	Violet and white	June	2-3 ft	(60-90 cm)
Iris laevigata 'Rose Queen'	Pink	June	2-3 ft	(60-90 cm)
Iris laevigata 'Variegata'	Blue/variegated foliage	June	2-3 ft	(60-90 cm)
Iris pseudacorus	Yellow	June	2½-3 ft	(75-90 cm)
Iris pseudacorus var. *bastardi*	Primrose	June	2½-3 ft	(75-90 cm)
Iris pseudacorus 'Variegata'	Yellow/variegated foliage	June	2½ ft	(75 cm)
Iris versicolor	Violet and purple	June	2-2½ ft	(60-75 cm)
Iris versicolor 'Kermesina'	Deep plum	June	2-2½ ft	(60-75 cm)

Appendix I

Name	Flower Colour	Flowering Period	Height	
Juncus effusus 'Spiralis'	Brown	June-July	1 ft 2 in-1½ ft	(35-45 cm)
Juncus effusus 'Vittatus'	Brown/ variegated foliage	June-July	1 ft 2 in-1½ ft	(35-45 cm)
Ludwigia palustris	Insig- nificant/ handsome foliage	–	1 ft	(30 cm)
Mentha aquatica	Lilac-pink	July-Sept	1-1½ ft	(30-45 cm)
Menyanthes trifoliata	White or pinkish	April-May	8 in-1 ft	(20-30 cm)
Mimulus luteus	Yellow	June-Aug	8 in-1 ft	(20-30 cm)
Mimulus ringens	Blue	June-Aug	1½ ft	(45 cm)
Mimulus 'Bonfire'	Red	June-Aug	8 in-1 ft	(20-30 cm)
Mimulus 'Highland Pink'	Pink	June-Aug	6 in	(15 cm)
Mimulus 'Highland Red'	Red	June-Aug	6 in	(15 cm)
Mimulus 'Hose in Hose'	Yellow, double	June-Aug	8 in-1 ft	(20-30 cm)
Mimulus 'Monarch Strain'	Mixed	June-Aug	8 in-1 ft	(20-30 cm)
Mimulus 'Queen's Prize'	Mixed	June-Aug	8 in-1 ft	(20-30 cm)
Mimulus 'Whitecroft Scarlet'	Scarlet	June-Aug	4 in	(10 cm)
Myosotis scorpioides	Blue	May-July	8 in	(20 cm)
Narthecium ossifragum	Yellow	July-Sept	10 in-1 ft 2 in	(25-35 cm)
Peltandra alba	White	June-July	1½ ft	(45 cm)
Peltandra virginica	Green	June-July	1½-2 ft	(45-60 cm)
Pontederia cordata	Blue	Aug-Sept	2-3 ft	(60-90 cm)
Preslia cervina	Blue	June-Aug	1 ft	(30 cm)
Ranunculus flammula	Yellow	May-July	10 in-1 ft 2 in	(25-35 cm)
Ranunculus lingua	Yellow	May-June	2-3 ft	(60-90 cm)
Ranunculus lingua 'Grandiflora'	Yellow	May-June	2-3 ft	(60-90 cm)
Sagittaria japonica	White	July-Sept	1½-2 ft	(45-60 cm)
Sagittaria japonica 'Flore-Pleno'	White, double	July-Sept	1½-2 ft	(45-60 cm)
Sagittaria latifolia	White	July-Sept	4-5 ft	(1 m 20 cm-1 m 50 cm)
Sagittaria sagittifolia	White	July-Sept	1½-2 ft	(45-60 cm)
Saururus cernuus	White	June-July	1 ft	(30 cm)
Scirpus lacustris	Reddish- brown	July	2-3 ft	(60-90 cm)
Scirpus tabernaemontani	Reddish- brown	July	2-4 ft	(60 cm-1 m 20 cm)
Scirpus tabernaemontani 'Albescens'	Reddish- brown/ white foliage	July	2-3 ft	(60-90 cm)
Scirpus tabernaemontani 'Zebrinus'	Reddish- brown	July	2-2½ ft	(60-75 cm)
Sparganium ramosum	Greenish	June-Aug	1 ft 8 in-3 ft	(50-90 cm)
Typha angustifolia	Brown	Aug-Sept	6 ft	(1 m 80 cm)
Typha latifolia	Brown	Aug-Sept	6 ft	(1 m 80 cm)
Typha laxmannii	Brown	Aug-Sept	3 ft-3 ft 3 in	(90 cm-1 m)
Typha minima	Brown	Aug-Sept	1½ ft	(45 cm)
Veronica beccabunga	Blue	June-Sept	6-8 in	(15-20 cm)

All the following floating plants grow in a sufficient depth of water to allow them to float freely.

Name	Flower Colour	Flowering Period
Azolla caroliniana	–	No flowers
Azolla filiculoides	–	No flowers
Hydrocharis morsus-ranae	White	June-Aug
Lemna trisulca	–	Insignificant
Stratiotes aloides	White	June-Aug
Trapa natans	White	June-Aug
Utricularia intermedia	Yellow	July
Utricularia minor	Yellow	July
Utricularia vulgaris	Yellow	July

All submerged oxygenating plants will grow in water depths between 8 in-1 ft 8 in (20-50 cm). Although most produce flowers few are of significance.

Name	Characteristics
Apium inundatum	Fresh green foliage/white flowers
Callitriche hermaphroditica	Cress-like foliage
Callitriche platycarpa	Cress-like foliage
Callitriche stagnalis	Cress-like foliage
Ceratophyllum demersum	Bristly green foliage
Ceratophyllum submersum	Bristly green foliage
Chara aspera	Green hairy foliage
Eleocharis acicularis	Grass-like leaves
Elodea canadensis	Dark green curled leaves
Fontinalis antipyretica	Dark green mossy foliage
Fontinalis gracilis	Dark green mossy foliage
Hottonia inflata	Light green divided foliage
Hottonia palustris	Light green divided foliage
Isoetes lacustris	Dark green quill-like leaves
Lagarosiphon major	Dark green crispy foliage
Lobelia dortmanna	Erect foliage/lavender flowers
Myriophyllum spicatum	Green filigree foliage
Myriophyllum verticillatum	Green filigree foliage
Oenanthe fluviatilis	Carrot-like foliage
Potomogeton crispus	Bronze-green translucent foliage
Potomogeton pectinatus	Bronze-green grassy leaves

Appendix I

Name	Characteristics
Ranunculus aquatilis	Green filigree foliage/white flowers
Tillaea recurva	Hard green foliage/small white flowers

Bog Garden Plants

Plants for moist positions beside pools and streams.

Name	Flower Colour	Flowering Period	Height	
Aconitum napellus	Dark blue	June-July	5 ft	(1 m 50 cm)
Aconitum napellus bicolor	Blue and white	June-July	2-3 ft	(60-90 cm)
Aconitum 'Bressingham Spire'	Dark blue	June-July	2-2$\frac{1}{2}$ ft	(60-75 cm)
Ajuga reptans 'Multicolor'	Blue/pink and cream foliage	May-July	6 in	(15 cm)
Ajuga reptans 'Purpurea'	Blue/ purplish foliage	May-July	6 in	(15 cm)
Anthericum liliago	White	May-July	2 ft	(60 cm)
Anthericum liliastrum major	White	May-July	2$\frac{1}{2}$ ft	(75 cm)
Aruncus sylvester	Creamy-white	July-Aug	4-5 ft	(1 m 20 cm-1 m 50 cm)
Aruncus sylvester 'Kneiffi'	Creamy-white	July-Aug	3 ft	(90 cm)
Asclepias incarnata	Rose-pink	June-July	3 ft 3 in-4 ft	(1 m-1 m 20 cm)
Aster puniceus	Lilac	Sept	3 ft	(90 cm)
Astilbe crispa 'Lilliput'	Pink	July	6 in	(15 cm)
Astilbe crispa 'Perkeo'	Pink	July-Aug	6 in	(15 cm)
Astilbe 'Fanal'	Red	July-Aug	2$\frac{1}{2}$ ft	(75 cm)
Astilbe 'Peach Blossom'	Soft pink	July-Aug	2$\frac{1}{2}$ ft	(75 cm)
Astilbe 'Red Sentinel'	Red	July-Aug	2$\frac{1}{2}$ ft	(75 cm)
Astilbe 'White Gloria'	White	July-Aug	2$\frac{1}{2}$ ft	(75 cm)
Bupthalmum speciosum	Yellow	June-Aug	4 ft	(1 m 20 cm)
Cardamine pratensis	Rosy-lilac	April	1 ft	(30 cm)
Cardamine pratensis flore-plena	Rosy-lilac	April	1 ft	(30 cm)
Eupatorium purpureum	Purple	July-Sept	4 ft	(1 m 20 cm)
Euphorbia palustris	Yellow-green	June-July	3 ft	(90 cm)
Filipendula hexapetala	Creamy-white	June-July	2 ft	(60 cm)
Filipendula hexapetala flore-pleno	Creamy-white	June-July	1 ft 4 in-2 ft	(40-60 cm)
Filipendula palmata	Pale pink	June-Aug	3 ft	(90 cm)
Filipendula ulmaria	Creamy-white	June-July	3 ft-3 ft 3 in	(90 cm-1 m)

Name	Flower Colour	Flowering Period	Height	
Filipendula ulmaria 'Aurea'	Creamy-white/ golden foliage	June-July	2½ ft-3 ft	(75-90 cm)
Gunnera manicata	Reddish-green	July-Sept	6 ft 6 in-8 ft	(2 m-2 m 40 cm)
Hemerocallis 'Hyperion'	Lemon-yellow	June-July	3 ft	(90 cm)
Hemerocallis 'Mikado'	Orange	June-July	2-3 ft	(60-90 cm)
Hemerocallis 'Pink Charm'	Pink	June-July	1 ft 8 in-2 ft	(50-60 cm)
Hosta fortunei	Lilac	June-July	1-1½ ft	(30-45 cm)
Hosta glauca	Pale lilac	June-July	1 ft-1 ft 8 in	(30-50 cm)
Hosta glauca 'Robusta'	Pale lilac	June-July	1 ft 2 in-1 ft 10 in	(35-55 cm)
Hosta lancifolia	Purple	July-Aug	1 ft 2 in-1 ft 4 in	(35-40 cm)
Hosta lancifolia 'Aurea'	Purple/ golden foliage	July-Aug	1 ft	(30 cm)
Hosta lancifolia 'Fortis'	Purple	July-Aug	1 ft 2 in-1 ft 4 in	(35-40 cm)
Hosta 'Thomas Hogg'	Pale purple/ green and white foliage	June-July	1½ ft	(45 cm)
Hosta undulata medio-variegata	Lavender/ cream and green foliage	July-Aug	1 ft	(30 cm)
Iris aurea	Golden-yellow	June-July	4 ft	(1 m 20 cm)
Iris bulleyana	Purple-blue	June	1 ft 4 in	(40 cm)
Iris chrysographes	Violet-purple	June	1 ft 4 in-2 ft	(40-60 cm)
Iris kaempferi	Blue	June-July	2-2½ ft	(60-75 cm)
Iris kaempferi 'Blue Heaven'	Purple-blue	June-July	2-2½ ft	(60-75 cm)
Iris kaempferi 'Higo' strain	Mixed colours	June-July	2-2½ ft	(60-75 cm)
Iris kaempferi 'Landscape at Dawn'	Rose-lavender	June-July	2-2½ ft	(60-75 cm)
Iris kaempferi 'Mandarin'	Violet	June-July	2-2½ ft	(60-75 cm)
Iris kaempferi 'Tokyo'	Mixed colours	June-July	2-2½ ft	(60-75 cm)
Iris kaempferi 'Variegata'	Blue/ variegated foliage	June-July	2-2½ ft	(60-75 cm)
Iris ochroleuca	White and yellow	June-July	5 ft	(1 m 50 cm)
Iris sibirica	Blue	June	2½-3 ft	(75-90 cm)
Iris sibirica 'Emperor'	Deep violet-blue	June	2½-3 ft	(75-90 cm)

Name	Flower Colour	Flowering Period	Height	
Iris sibirica 'Ottawa'	Deep violet	June	$2\frac{1}{2}$-3 ft	(75-90 cm)
Iris sibirica 'Perry's Blue'	Blue	June	$2\frac{1}{2}$-3 ft	(75-90 cm)
Iris sibirica 'Perry's Pygmy'	Blue	June	1 ft 2 in	(35 cm)
Iris sibirica 'Snow Queen'	White	June	$2\frac{1}{2}$-3 ft	(75-90 cm)
Ligularia clivorum	Orange	Aug-Sept	3-4 ft	(90 cm-1 m 20 cm)
Ligularia clivorum 'Desdemona'	Yellow	Aug-Sept	3-4 ft	(90 cm-1 m 20 cm)
Ligularia clivorum 'Orange Queen'	Orange	Aug-Sept	3-4 ft	(90 cm-1 m 20 cm)
Ligularia clivorum 'Othello'	Orange	Aug-Sept	3-4 ft	(90 cm-1 m 20 cm)
Lobelia cardinalis	Red	Aug-Sept	2ft 4 in-3 ft	(70-90 cm)
Lobelia fulgens	Red	Aug-Sept	$2\frac{1}{2}$-3 ft	(75-90 cm)
Lobelia vedrariensis	Violet	Aug-Sept	3 ft 3 in	(1 m)
Lysichitum americanum	Yellow	April	3 ft	(90 cm)
Lysichitum camtschatense	White	April	$2\frac{1}{2}$-3 ft	(75-90 cm)
Lysimachia nummularia	Yellow	June-July	2 in	(5 cm)
Lysimachia nummularia 'Aurea'	Yellow/ golden foliage	June-July	2 in	(5 cm)
Lysimachia punctata	Yellow	June-July	2-3 ft	(60-90 cm)
Lythrum salicaria	Purple	July-Sept	4 ft	(1 m 20 cm)
Lythrum salicaria 'Lady Sackville'	Rose-pink	July-Sept	$2\frac{1}{2}$ ft-3 ft 3 in	(75 cm-1 m)
Lythrum salicaria 'Robert'	Pink	July-Sept	$2\frac{1}{2}$ ft-3 ft 3 in	(75 cm-1 m)
Lythrum salicaria 'The Beacon'	Rose-red	July-Sept	$2\frac{1}{2}$ ft-3 ft 3 in	(75 cm-1 m)
Lythrum virgatum	Purple-red	July-Sept	$1\frac{1}{2}$ ft	(45 cm)
Lythrum virgatum 'Dropmore Purple'	Purple	July-Sept	$1\frac{1}{2}$ ft	(45 cm)
Lythrum virgatum 'Rose Queen'	Deep rose	July-Sept	$1\frac{1}{2}$ ft	(45 cm)
Mimulus cardinalis	Red	July-Sept	$1\frac{1}{2}$-2 ft	(45-60 cm)
Parnassia palustris	Snow-white	May-July	6 in-1 ft	(15-30 cm)
Peltiphyllum peltatum	Pink	April	$1\frac{1}{2}$ ft	(45 cm)
Petasites japonicus	White	Feb-March	5 ft	(1 m 50 cm)
Phormium tenax	Reddish foliage	July-Sept	3 ft 3 in-5 ft	(1 m-1 m 50 cm)
Phormium tenax atropurpurea	Reddish/ purplish foliage	July-Sept	3 ft 3in	(1 m)
Phormium tenax variegata	Reddish/ variegated foliage	July-Sept	3 ft 3 in	(1 m)
Primula 'Asthore Hybrids'	Mixed colours	May	$1\frac{1}{2}$ ft	(45 cm)
Primula aurantiaca	Orange-yellow	May	$2\frac{1}{2}$ ft	(75 cm)
Primula beesiana	Rosy-purple	June-July	2 ft	(60 cm)

Name	Flower Colour	Flowering Period	Height	
Primula bulleyana	Orange-yellow	June-July	2½ ft	(75 cm)
Primula chungensis	Pale orange	June	1 ft	(30 cm)
Primula denticulata	Lilac-blue	March-April	1 ft	(30 cm)
Primula denticulata alba	White	March-April	1 ft	(30 cm)
Primula denticulata cashmireana	Lilac-purple	March-April	1 ft	(30 cm)
Primula florindae	Yellow	June-Aug	3 ft	(90 cm)
Primula helodoxa	Yellow	July-Aug	3 ft	(90 cm)
Primula japonica	Crimson	May-June	2 ft	(60 cm)
Primula japonica 'Miller's Crimson'	Crimson	May-June	2 ft	(60 cm)
Primula japonica 'Postford White'	White	May-June	2 ft	(60 cm)
Primula microdonta alpicola	Soft yellow	May-June	1½ ft	(45 cm)
Primula microdonta alpicola var. *violacea*	Violet-mauve	May-June	1½ ft	(45 cm)
Primula pulverulenta	Magenta	May-June	2 ft	(60 cm)
Primula pulverulenta 'Bartley Strain'	Buff or pink	May-June	2 ft	(60 cm)
Primula rosea	Rose-pink	March-April	6-8 in	(15-20 cm)
Primula rosea grandiflora	Rose-pink	March-April	6-8 in	(15-20 cm)
Primula rosea 'Delight'	Rose-pink	March-April	6-8 in	(15-20 cm)
Primula secundiflora	Rose-red	May-June	1 ft	(30 cm)
Primula sikkimensis	Yellow	June-July	1 ft	(30 cm)
Primula viali	Lilac and red	June	1 ft	(30 cm)
Primula waltoni	Port wine	July-Aug	1½ ft	(45 cm)
Rheum palmatum	Creamy-white	May-July	6 ft	(1 m 80 cm)
Rheum palmatum 'Bowles Crimson'	Crimson	May-July	6 ft	(1 m 80 cm)
Rheum palmatum tanguticum	Deep rose	May-July	6 ft	(1 m 80 cm)
Rodgersia aesculifolia	Creamy-white	June-July	3 ft	(90 cm)
Rodgersia pinnata	Rose-pink	June-July	3 ft	(90 cm)
Rodgersia tabularis	Creamy-white	June-July	3 ft	(90 cm)
Schizostylis coccinea	Red	Oct-Nov	1 ft-1 ft 8 in	(30-50 cm)
Schizostylis coccinea 'Grandiflora'	Red	Oct-Nov	1 ft-1 ft 8 in	(30-50 cm)
Schizostylis coccinea 'Mrs Hegarty'	Rose-pink	Oct-Nov	1 ft-1 ft 8 in	(30-50 cm)
Symplocarpus foetidus	Purple	April-May	2½-3 ft	(75-90 cm)
Trollius asiaticus	Orange	April-June	2-2½ ft	(60-75 cm)
Trollius europaeus	Yellow	April-June	2-2½ ft	(60-75 cm)
Trollius 'Canary Bird'	Yellow	April-June	2-2½ ft	(60-75 cm)
Trollius 'Fire Globe'	Orange	April-June	2-2½ ft	(60-75 cm)
Trollius 'Orange Princess'	Orange	April-June	2-2½ ft	(60-75 cm)

Appendix I

Ferns for the Bog Garden

Name	Characteristics	Height	
Dryopteris cristata	Pale green, creeping	1 ft	(30 cm)
Dryopteris palustris	Finely cut fronds, creeping	2-3 ft	(60-90 cm)
Matteucia struthiopteris	Bright green shuttlecocks	3 ft-3 ft 3 in	(90 cm-1 m)
Onoclea sensibilis	Rose-pink fronds, changing to green	2½-3 ft	(45-60 cm)
Osmunda regalis	Green fronds, turning bronze	4-5 ft	(1 m 20-1 m 80 cm)
Osmunda regalis 'Cristata'	Tassellated fronds	3 ft 3 in	(1 m)
Osmunda regalis 'Purpurescens'	Purplish-green fronds	3 ft 3 in- 5ft	(1 m-1 m 50 cm)
Osmunda regalis 'Undulata'	Crimpled and crested fronds	3 ft 3 in	(1 m)
Woodwardia virginica	Olive-green fronds	2 ft	(60 cm)

Tender Aquatics — Tropical Waterlilies

Day Blooming

Name	Flower Colour	Depth of Water	
Nymphaea capensis	Blue	1½-2½ ft	(45-75 cm)
Nymphaea capensis var. *zanzibariensis*	Blue	1½-2½ ft	(45-75 cm)
Nymphaea coerulea	Blue	1½-2½ ft	(45-75 cm)
Nymphaea colorata	Purple or lilac	1½-2½ ft	(45-75 cm)
Nymphaea flavo-virens	White	1½-2½ ft	(45-75 cm)
Nymphaea heudelotii	Bluish-white	1 ft	(30 cm)
Nymphaea mexicana	Canary-yellow	6 in-1 ft	(15-30 cm)
Nymphaea stellata	Blue or white	1½-2½ ft	(45-75 cm)
Nymphaea stellata var. *versicolor*	Grown for foliage	1½-2½ ft	(45-75 cm)
Nymphaea stellata 'Berlin'	Blue	1½-2½ ft	(45-75 cm)
Nymphaea 'August Koch'	Mid-blue	1½-2½ ft	(45-75 cm)
Nymphaea 'Blue Beauty'	Blue	1½-3 ft	(45-90 cm)
Nymphaea 'Colonel Lindberg'	Deep blue	1½-2½ ft	(45-75 cm)
Nymphaea 'Daubeniana'	Blue	6 in	(15 cm)
Nymphaea 'General Pershing'	Deep pink	1½-2½ ft	(45-75 cm)
Nymphaea 'Green Smoke'	Chartreuse	1½-2½ ft	(45-75 cm)
Nymphaea 'Independence'	Rose-pink	1½-2½ ft	(45-75 cm)
Nymphaea 'Leading Lady'	Peach	2½ ft-3 ft 3 in	(75 cm-1 m)
Nymphaea 'Margaret Mary'	Blue	1 ft	(30 cm)
Nymphaea 'Midnight'	Purple	1-2 ft	(30-60 cm)
Nymphaea 'Mrs George H. Pring'	Creamy-white	1½-2½ ft	(45-75 cm)
Nymphaea 'Panama Pacific'	Purplish-blue	1½-2½ ft	(45-75 cm)
Nymphaea 'Patricia'	Crimson	1-1½ ft	(30-45 cm)

158

Name	Flower Colour	Depth of Water	
Nymphaea 'Pride of Winterhaven'	Fuchsia-lavender	1½-2½ ft	(45-75 cm)
Nymphaea 'St Louis'	Canary-yellow	1½-2½ ft	(45-75 cm)

Night Blooming

Name	Flower Colour	Depth of Water	
Nymphaea amazonum	Creamy-white	1½-2 ft	(45-60 cm)
Nymphaea lotus	White	1½-2½ ft	(45-75 cm)
Nymphaea rubra	Deep red	1½-2½ ft	(45-75 cm)
Nymphaea rubra 'Rosea'	Red	1½-2½ ft	(45-75 cm)
Nymphaea 'B.C. Berry'	Amaranth-purple	1½-2½ ft	(45-75 cm)
Nymphaea 'Emily Grant Hutchings'	Deep pinkish-red	1½-2½ ft	(45-75 cm)
Nymphaea 'Janice Ruth'	White	1-1½ ft	(30-45 cm)
Nymphaea 'Maroon Beauty'	Maroon	1½-2½ ft	(45-75 cm)
Nymphaea 'Missouri'	White	2½ ft-3 ft 3 in	(75 cm-1 m)
Nymphaea 'Pride of California'	Deep red	1½-2½ ft	(45-75 cm)
Nymphaea 'Trudy Slocum'	White	1½-2½ ft	(45-75 cm)

All the *Nelumbos* require a depth of water between 9 in-1 ft (23-30 cm).

Sacred Lotus (Nelumbos)

Name	Flower Colour	Height	
Nelumbo nucifera	Rose-pink	6 ft-7 ft 2 in	(1 m 80 cm-2 m 15 cm)
Nelumbo nucifera var. *alba*	White	6 ft-7 ft 2 in	(1 m 80 cm-2 m 15 cm)
Nelumbo pentapetala	Pale yellow	3 ft	(90 cm)
Nelumbo pentapetala var. *flavescens*	Pale yellow	3 ft	(90 cm)
Nelumbo 'Chawan Basu'	White-edged pink	1 ft-1 ft 8 in	(30-50 cm)
Nelumbo 'Kermesina'	Double red	3 ft 3 in-5 ft	(1 m-1 m 50 cm)
Nelumbo 'Lily Pons'	Salmon-pink	3 ft 3 in-5 ft	(1 m-1 m 50 cm)
Nelumbo 'Mrs Perry D. Slocum'	Double, rose-pink to yellow	5-6 ft	(1 m 50 cm-1 m 80 cm)
Nelumbo 'Momo Botan'	Double carmine	1 ft-1 ft 4 in	(30-40 cm)
Nelumbo 'Osiris'	Rose-pink	3 ft 3 in-5 ft	(1 m-1 m 50 cm)
Nelumbo 'Pygmaea Alba'	White	1 ft	(30 cm)
Nelumbo 'Pygmaea Alba Plena'	Double white	1 ft	(30 cm)
Nelumbo 'Pygmaea Rosea'	Rose-pink	1 ft	(30 cm)

Appendix I

Other Tender Aquatics

This section comprises a selection of fine floating and marginal subjects in the order in which they appear in the text.

Name	Flower Colour	Habit	Height	
Ceratopteris pteridoides	Non-flowering	Floating	2½-4 in	(7-10 cm)
Ceratopteris thalictroides	Non-flowering	Floating	2½-4 in	(7-10 cm)
Eichornia crassipes	Blue-lilac	Floating	6-8 in	(15-20 cm)
Hydrocleys commersonii	Golden-yellow	Floating	2½-4 in	(7-10 cm)
Salvinia auriculata	Non-flowering	Floating	¾ in	(2 cm)
Thalia dealbata	Purple	Marginal	5 ft	(1 m 50 cm)
Zantedeschia aethiopica	White	Marginal	3 ft	(90 cm)
Zantedeschia aethiopica 'Crowborough'	White	Marginal	2½ ft	(75 cm)

Tender Submerged Aquatics

Name	Characteristics
Anubias lanceolata	Broad shiny leaves
Aponogeton crispus	Translucent leaves, feathery flowers
Aponogeton fenestralis	Lacy foliage
Aponogeton ulvaceous	Translucent foliage
Cabomba aquatica	Feathery submerged foliage, kidney-shaped floating leaves
Cabomba caroliniana	Feathery green foliage
Cabomba caroliniana 'Rosaefolia'	Feathery rose-pink foliage
Cryptocoryne cordata	Yellowish-green cordate foliage
Echinodorus intermedius	Sword-like leaves
Echinodorus radicans	Short-lanceolate leaves
Egeria densa	Curly green leaves
Heteranthera graminea	Curly green foliage/yellow blossoms
Heteranthera zosteraefolia	Curly green foliage/blue flowers
Hygrophila polysperma	Green foliage/red stems
Ludwigia mulertii	Bronze-green leaves, purple undersides
Marsilea quadrifolia	Clover-like leaves
Myriophyllum hippuroides	Green feathery foliage
Myriophyllum scabratum	Reddish-bronze feathery foliage
Riccia fluitans	Green starry foliage
Sagittaria lorata	Narrow green leaves/white flowers
Sagittaria subulata	Grassy foliage
Vallisnaria spiralis	Tape-like foliage
Vallisnaria spiralis 'Torta'	Twisted tape-like foliage

Nursery Suppliers

Most of the listed suppliers provide a full range of everything that the water gardener requires — including pools, plants and fish.

Bennetts Waterlily Farm
Chickerell
Weymouth
Dorset

J. and F. Mimmack
Woodholme Nursery
Goatsmoor Lane
Stock
Essex

Jackamoors Hardy Plant
Farm
Theobalds Park Road
Enfield
Middlesex

Lotus Water Garden
Products Ltd
Chesham
Bucks

P. and A. Plant Supplies Ltd
The Nursery
Sutton
Norfolk

Stapeley Water Gardens Ltd
Stapeley
Nantwich
Cheshire CW5 7JL

Wildwoods Water Garden
Centre
Theobalds Park Road
Enfield
Middlesex

Great Britain

Slocum Water Gardens
1101 Cypress Gardens Road
Winter Haven, Florida 33880

Van Ness Water Gardens
2460 North Euclid Avenue
Upland, California 91786

William Tricker Inc
74 Allendale Avenue
PO Box 398
Saddle River, NJ 07458

USA

France | Etablissements Latour | R. Bezançon
Marliac | 15 Avenue du Raincy
31 Allees de Tourny | 94 Saint Maur
Bordeaux

Italy | Giardini Di Marignolle
Via Di Marignolle 69
50124 Firenze

New Zealand | Liliponds
Murray L Williams
Eskdale RD2
Napier

Useful Information

Rectangular Pools (or Aquaria)

Multiply length by width by depth (all in feet) to obtain volume in cubic feet. Multiply this by 6.25 to give the capacity in gallons.

Circular Pools

Multiply depth in feet by the square of the diameter in feet by 4.9 to give approximate gallonage.

Capacity of rectangular pools one foot average depth in Imperial gallons.

Breadth (ft)	Length (ft)						
	2	4	6	8	10	12	16
2	25	50	75	100	125	150	200
3	38	75	112	150	186	275	300
4	50	100	150	200	250	300	400
5	62	125	186	250	310	375	500
6	75	150	225	300	375	450	600

**Easy
Reference
Table for
Circular Pools**

Capacity of circular garden pools in Imperial gallons.

Diameter (ft)	Average Depth of Water in Inches				
	12	18	24	30	36
4	78	117	156	195	234
6	176	264	352	440	528
8	313	470	626	783	939
10	489	734	978	1,223	1,467
12	705	1,058	1,410	1,763	2,115

**Volume —
Rate of Flow**

An important factor when installing a fountain or waterfall.

Gallons per Minute	Gallons per Hour	Litres per Minute	Litres per Hour
1	60	4.55	272.7
2	120	9.09	545.5
3	180	13.64	818.3
4	240	18.18	1,091
5	300	22.73	1,363
6	360	27.27	1,636
7	420	31.82	1,909
8	480	36.37	2,182
9	540	40.91	2,454
10	600	45.46	2,727
11	660	50.00	3,000
12	720	54.55	3,273
13	780	59.10	3,545
14	840	63.64	3,818
15	900	68.10	4,091
16	960	72.74	4,364
17	1,020	77.28	4,636
18	1,080	81.83	4,909
19	1,140	86.38	5,182
20	1,200	90.92	5,455

One Imperial gallon of water occupies 0.16 cubic feet, and weighs 10 lb.

One US gallon is equivalent to 0.83268 Imperial gallons, and weighs 8.3 lb.

One cubic foot of water is equivalent to 6.24 Imperial gallons or 28.3 litres, and weighs 62.32 lb.

One Imperial gallon equals 160 fluid ounces or 4.546 litres.

One litre equals 1.76 Imperial pints or 0.22 Imperial gallons or 35.196 fluid ounces.

One litre equals 0.264 US gallons.

4 teaspoonsful are equivalent to 2 dessertspoonsful, 1 tablespoonful or $\frac{1}{2}$ ounce.

Index

Achyla 138
Aconitum napellus 64
A.n. bicolor 65
A.n. 'Bressingham Spire' 64
Acorus calamus 42
A.c. 'Variegatus' 42
A. gramineus 43
A.g. 'Variegatus' 43
Ajuga reptans 65
A.r. 'Multicolor' 65
A.r. 'Purpurea' 65
Alisma parviflora 43
A. plantago-aquatica 43
A. ranunculoides 43
Amazon Sword Plant 94
Ameiurus nebulosus 104
Anadonta cygnea 113
Anchor Worm 134
Anthericum liliago 65
A. liliastrum major 65
Anubias lanceolata 93
Apium inundatum 57
Aponogeton crispus 93
A. distachyus 39, 40
A. fenestralis 93
A. ulvaceous 94
Aquatic plant diseases 134
Aquatic plant pests 131
Aquatic propagation 126
Argulus 135
Arrow Arum 49
Arrowhead 50, 51, 127
Arum Lily 92
Aruncus 'Kneiffi' 65
Aruncus sylvester 65
Asclepias incarnata 65
Aster puniceus 65
Astilbe astiboides 65
A. crispa 'Lilliput' 66
A. crispa 'Perkeo' 66
A. 'Fanal' 66
A. japonica 65
A. 'Peach Blossom' 66
A. 'Red Sentinel' 66
A. thunbergii 65

A. 'White Gloria' 66
Azolla caroliniana 61, 92
A. filiculoides 61

Balance, loss of 142
Baldellia ranunculoides 43
Bass 106
Beetle: Great Diving 135; Great Silver 136; Waterlily 133; Whirligig 137
Bitterling 98, 128
Black Moor 100, 101
Bladderwort: Greater 62; Intermediate 62
Bog Arum 44, 127
Bog Asphodel 49
Bog Bean 48
Bog Garden Construction 63
Brandy Bottle 39
Brooklime 52, 127
Brown Bullhead 105
Buck Bean 48
Bufo bufo bufo 115
Bugle 65
Bulrush 51
Bulrush, Glaucous 51
Bupthalmum speciosum 66
Bur Reed 52
Butomus umbellatus 43
Butterbur 72

Cabomba aquatica 94
C. caroliniana 94
C.c. 'Rosaefolia' 94
Caddis Flies 132
Calla palustris 44
Callitriche autumnalis 57
C. platycarpa 57
C. stagnalis 57
C. verna 57
Caltha palustris 44
C.p. alba 44
C. leptosepala 44
C. polypetala 44
Canadian Pondweed 58

Carassius auratus auratus 99
C. carassius 99
Cardamine pratensis 66
C.p. flore-plena 66
Cardinal Monkey Flower 72
Carex pendula 45
C. riparia 45
C.r. 'Aurea' 45
C.r. 'Variegata' 45
Carp: Band 98; Bronze 98; Chinese
    Red 98; Common 98; Crucian 99;
    Higoi 98, 108; Ki-ogen 102; Koi
    102, 108; Leather 98; Mirror 98;
    Nishiki Koi 102; Sanke 102; Shiro-
    ogen 102
Cataract 141
Catfish 104, 128
Ceratophyllum demersum 57
C. submersum 57
Ceratopteris pteridoides 91
C. thalictroides 91
Cercosporae 134
Chara aspera 57, 58
Chilodonella 139
China Mark Moth: Beautiful 131;
    Brown 131
Chlorine damage 141
Clemmys leprosa 116
Constipation 142
Coontail 57
Corkscrew Rush 47
Costia 139
Cotton Grass 46; Broad Leafed 46
Crassula recurva 61
Creeping Jenny 71
Cricotopus ornatus 132
Cryptocoryne cordata 94
Crystalwort 96
Cuckoo Flower 66
Cyclochaete 139
Cyperus alternifolius 45
C. eragrostis 45
C. longus 45
C. vegetus 45
Cyprinus carpio 98

Dace 99, 103
Dactylogyrus 139
Damasonium alisma 45
D. stellatum 45
Daylily 66
Dragonflies 134
Dropsy 138
Dropwort 66
Dryopteris cristata 77
D. palustris 77
Duckweed, Ivy-leafed 61
Dytiscus marginalis 135

Echinodorus intermedius 94

E. radicans 94
Egeria densa 94, 95
Eichornia crassipes 91
Elassoma 106
Eleocharis acicularis 58
Elodea canadensis 58
E. crispa 59
E. densa 94
Emys blandingii 116
E. orbicularis 116
Enneacanthos 106
Eriophorum angustifolium 46
E. latifolium 46
E. polystachyon 46
Eupatorium purpureum 66
Euphorbia palustris 66

Fairy Moss 61
False Goat's Beard 65
False Leaf-mining Midge 132
False Loosestrife 47
Fantail 100, 101
Fanwort 94
Fern: Crested Buckler 77; Marsh
    Buckler 77; Ostrich Feather 77;
    Royal 78; Sensitive 77; Virginian
    Chain 78
Filipendula hexapetala 66
F.h. flore-pleno 66
F. palmata 66
F. ulmaria 66
F. ulmaria 'Aurea' 67
Fin Rot 138
Fish: Breeding 128; Diseases 138;
    Feeding 110; Louse 135;
    Ornamental 97; Pests 134;
    Scavenging 104
Floating Fern 91
Flowering Rush 43
Foil Plant 95
Fontinalis antipyretica 58
F. gracilis 58
Fountains 6-10
Frog: Common 114; Edible 114;
    Marsh 114
Frogbit 61
Fungus 138

Galerucella nymphaea 133
Gill Flukes 139
Globe Flower 77
Glyceria aquatica 'Variegata' 46
Goat's Beard 65
Gobio gobio 107
Goldfish 99, 100, 108; Celestial 101,
    102; Comet 100; Fantail 100, 101;
    Lionhead 101, 102; Oranda 101,
    102; Telescope 101; Veiltail 101
Grass of Parnassus 72
Gudgeon 107

Index

Gunnera manicata 67
Gyrodactylus 139

Hair Grass 58
Halesus radiatus 132
Hemerocallis flava 68
H. fulva 68
H. 'Hyperion' 68
H. 'Mikado' 68
H. 'Pink Charm' 67, 68
Heron 143
Heteranthera graminea 95
H. zosteraefolia 95
Himalayan Cowslip 74
Horned Pout 104
Hornwort 57, 127
Hosta fortunei 68
H. glauca 68
H. lancifolia 68
H.l. 'Aurea' 68
H.l. 'Fortis' 68
H. sieboldii 68
H.s. 'Robusta' 68
H. 'Thomas Hogg' 68
H. undulata medio-variegata 68
Hottonia inflata 59
H. palustris 59
Houttuynia cordata 46
H.c. 'Plena' 46
H. foetida 46
Hydra oligactis 136
H. viridissima 136
H. vulgaris 136
Hydrocharis morsus-ranae 61
Hydrocleys commersonii 92
Hydrous piceus 136
Hygrophila polysperma 95
Hypericum elodes 46

Ich 140, 141
Ichthyophthirius multifils 140, 141
Ictalyrus nebulosus 105
Idus idus 103
Isoetes lacustris 89
Iris aurea 68
I. bulleyana 69
I. chrysographes 69
I. kaempferi 46, 47, 69
I.k. 'Blue Heaven' 69
I.k. 'Higo' 69
I.k. 'Landscape at Dawn' 69
I.k. 'Mandarin' 69
I.k. 'Tokyo' 69
I.k. 'Variegata' 69
I. laevigata 46, 47
I.l. 'Alba' 46
I.l. 'Colchesteri' 46
I.l. 'Rose Queen' 46
I.l. 'Variegata' 47
I. ochroleuca 69

I. pseudacorus 47
I.p. var. *bastardi* 47
I.p. 'Gold Queen' 47
I.p. 'Variegata' 47
I. sibirica 69
I.s. 'Emperor' 69
I.s. 'Ottawa' 69
I.s. 'Perry's Blue' 69
I.s. 'Perry's Pygmy' 69
I.s. 'Snow Queen' 69
I. versicolor 47
I.v. 'Kermesina' 47
Ivy-leafed Duckweed 61

Joe-Pye-Weed 66
Juncus effusus 47
J.e. 'Spiralis' 47
J.e. 'Vittatus' 47

Kaffir Lily 77

Lagarosiphon major 59
Leeches 136; fish 136
Lemna trisulca 61
Lernaea carassii 134
Leuciscus leuciscus 99
Ligularia clivorum 70
L.c. 'Desdemona' 70
L.c. 'Orange Queen' 70
L.c. 'Othello' 70
Limnaea auricularia 113
L. peregrina 113
L. stagnalis 112
Limnephilus marmoratus 132
Limnocharis humboldtii 92
Lizards' Tail 51
Lobelia cardinalis 70
L. dortmanna 59
L. fulgens 70
L. × *vedrariensis* 70
Loosestrife: False 47; Purple 72
Loss of balance 142
Lotus: American 89; Blue Nile 83;
    East Indian 89, 90; Eygptian 83;
    Sacred 89, 90; White Nile 86
Ludwigia mulertii 95
L. palustris 95
Lysichitum americanum 70, 71
L. camtschatense 70, 71
Lysimachia nummularia 70
L.n. 'Aurea' 71
L. punctata 71
Lythrum salicaria 72
L.s. 'Lady Sackville' 72
L.s. 'Robert' 72
L. virgatum 72
L.v. 'Dropmore Purple' 72
L.v. 'Rose Queen' 72

Madagascar Lace Plant 93

Marsh Hypericum 46
Marsh Marigold 20, 44, 127;
    Himalayan 44
Marsilea quadrifolia 95
Matteucia struthiopteris 77
Meadow Sweet 66
Medeka 106
Mentha aquatica 48
Menyanthes trifoliata 48
Mesogonistius 106
Milfoil: Spiked 60; Whorled 60
Milkweed Swamp 65
Mimulus 'Bonfire' 49
M. cardinalis 72
M. 'Highland Pink' 49
M. 'Highland Red' 49
M. 'Hose-in-Hose' 49
M. luteus 49
M. 'Monarch Strain' 49
M. 'Queen's Prize' 49
M. ringens 49
M. 'Tigrinus' 49
M. 'Whitecroft Scarlet' 49
Minnow 103
Monkshood 64
Musk 49
Mussels 112, 113; Painter's 98, 113;
    Swan 113
Mycobacterium tuberculosis 143
Myosotis palustris 49
M. scorpioides 49
Myriophyllum hippuroides 95
M. scabratum 95
M. spicatum 60
M. verticillatum 60

Narthecium ossifragum 49
Nelumbium luteum 89
N. speciosum 89
Nelumbo nucifera 88, 89, 90
N.n. var. *alba* 89
N.n. var. *alba striata* 89
N. pentapetala 89
N.p. var. *flavescens* 90
N. 'Chaw An Basu' 90
N. 'Chawan Basu' 90
N. 'Empress' 89
N. 'Kermesina' 90
N. 'Lilypons' 91
N. 'Momo Botan' 90
N. 'Osiris' 91
N. 'Perry D. Slocum' 91
N. 'Pygmaea Alba' 91
N. 'Pygmaea Alba Plena' 91
N. 'Pygmaea Rosea' 91
N. 'Shiroman' 89
Nepa cinerea 137
Newts: Common 115; Great Crestec
    115; Palmate 115
New Zealand Flax 73

Notonecta glauca 137
Nuphar advena 38
N. japonica 38
N. lutea 39
N. minimum 39
N. pumilum 39
N. rubrodisca 39
Nymphaea 'Aflame' 33
N. 'Alaska' 32
N. alba 29, 123
N. 'Albatross' 32
N. 'Amabilis' 32
N. amazonum 86
N. ampla 86
N. 'Andreana' 32
N. 'Arethusa' 32
N. 'Attraction' 32
N. 'August Koch' 84
N. 'Aurora' 32, 38
N. 'Baroness Orczy' 32
N. 'B.C. Berry' 87
N. 'Blue Beauty' 84
N. candida 30
N. capensis 83
N.c. var. *zanzibariensis* 83
N. caroliniana 30
N.c. 'Nivea' 30
N.c. 'Perfecta' 30
N.c. 'Rosea' 30
N. 'Charles De Meurville' 32
N. coerulea 2, 83
N. 'Colonel Lindberg' 84
N. colorata 81, 83
N. 'Comanche' 33
N. 'Conqueror' 33
N. 'Crystal White' 34
N. 'Daubeniana' 84
N. 'Ellisiana' 33
N. 'Emily Grant Hutchings' 87
N. 'Escarboucle' 33
N. 'Fabiola' 33
N. flava 83
N. flavo-virens 83
N. 'Froebeli' 33
N. 'Galatee' 34
N. 'General Pershing' 86
N. 'Gladstoniana' 34
N. 'Gloire de Temple Sur Lot' 34
N. 'Gloriosa' 34
N. 'Glory' 34
N. 'Golden Cup' 36
N. 'Gonnere' 34
N. gracilis 83
N. 'Graziella' 34
N. 'Green Smoke' 85
N. 'Hermine' 34
N. 'Hermione' 34
N. heudelotii 83
N. 'Independence' 85
N. 'Indiana' 34

Index

N. 'James Brydon' 34
N. 'Janice Ruth' 87
N. laydekeri 'Alba' 35
N.l. 'Fulgens' 35
N.l. 'Lilacea' 35
N.l. 'Purpurata' 35
N. 'Leading Lady' 85
N. lotus 2, 86
N. 'Louise' 35
N. 'Margaret Mary' 85
N. 'Marliac Flesh' 35
N. 'Marliac Pink' 36
N. 'Marliac Rose' 36
N. 'Marliac White' 35
N. 'Marliac Yellow' 36
N. marliacea 'Albida' 35
N.m. 'Carnea' 35, 36
N.m. 'Chromatella' 36
N.m. 'Flammea' 36
N.m. 'Rosea' 36
N. 'Maroon Beauty' 87
N. 'Mary Exquisita' 35
N. 'Masaniello' 36
N. 'Meteor' 36
N. mexicana 83
N. 'Midnight' 85
N. 'Missouri' 87
N. 'Mooreana' 37
N. 'Moorei' 37
N. 'Mrs George H. Pring' 85
N. 'Mrs Richmond' 37
N. 'Newton' 37
N. odorata 24, 30, 123
N.o. 'Eugene de Land' 30
N.o. 'Firecrest' 30, 31
N.o. 'Sulphurea' 30
N.o. 'Sulphurea Grandiflora' 30
N.o. 'Turicensis' 31
N.o. var. minor 30
N.o. var. rosea 30, 31
N.o. 'William B. Shaw' 31
N. 'Panama Pacific 85
N. 'Patricia' 86
N. 'Pearl of the Pool' 37
N. 'Pennsylvania' 84
N. 'Pink Marvel' 32
N. 'Pink Sensation' 37
N. 'Pride of California' 87
N. 'Pride of Winterhaven' 86
N. pygmaea 'Alba' 28, 37
N.p. 'Helvola' 37, 38
N.p. 'Rubra' 38
N. 'Pygmy Yellow' 37, 38
N. 'Rene Gerard' 38
N. 'Rose Arey' 38
N. rubra 87
N. rubra 'Rosea' 87
N. 'St Louis' 86
N. 'Sioux' 38
N. 'Somptuosa' 38

N. stellata 84
N.s. 'Berlin' 84
N.s. var. versicolor 84
N. 'Sunrise' 38
N. 'Tanganyika' 83
N. tetragona 2, 28, 31
N.t. 'Johann Pring' 31
N. 'Trudy Slocum' 87
N. tuberosa 24, 28, 31, 123
N.t. 'Richardsonii' 31
N.t. var. rosea 31
N. 'Virginalis' 38
N. zanzibariensis 83
Nymphoides peltata 40, 121
Nymphula nympheata 131
N. stagnata 131

Oenanthe fluviatilis 60
Onoclea sensibilis 77
Orectochilus villosus 137
Orfe: Golden 103, 108; Silver 103
Orontium aquaticum 40
Oryzias latipes 106
Osmunda regalis 78
O.r. 'Cristata' 78
O.r. 'Purpurescens' 78
O.r. 'Undulata' 78
Ovularis nymphaerum 134

Parnassia palustris 72
Peltandra alba 49
P. virginica 49
Peltiphyllum peltatum 72
Petasites japonicus 72
Phormium tenax 73
P.t. atropurpurea 73
P.t. variegata 73
Phoxinus phoxinus 103
Phytophthora 134
Pickerel Weed 49, 127
Piscicola geometra 136
Planorbis corneus 113
P.c. var. albus 113
P.c. var. rubra 113
Pond: Terrapin 116; Tortoise 116
Pond Lily: Dwarf 39; Japanese 38;
    Least Yellow 39; Red Disked 39
Pondweed: Curled 60; Fennel-leafed
    60
Pontederia cordata 49
Potamogeton crispus 60
P. pectinatus 60
Pool: concrete 17, 125; design 5; liner
    11, 124; natural 19; pre-shaped 15,
    125
Preslia cervina 50
Primula 'Asthore Hybrids' 73
P. aurantiaca 73
P. beesiana 73
P. bulleyana 73

Index

P. chungensis 74
P. denticulata 74
P.d. var. *alba* 74
P.d. var. *cashmireana* 74
P. florindae 74
P. helodoxa 74
P. japonica 75
P.j. 'Miller's Crimson' 75
P.j. 'Postford White' 75
P. littoniana 75
P. microdonta alpicola 75
P.m.a. var. *violacea* 75
P. pulverulenta 74, 75
P.p. 'Bartley Strain' 75
P. rosea 75
P. r. 'Delight' 75
P. r. grandiflora 75
P. secundiflora 75
P. sikkimensis 75
P. viali 75, 76
P. waltonii 75
Propagation: Aquatic Plants 126;
    Waterlilies 27, 81

Quillwort 59

Rana esculenta 114
R. ridibunda ridibunda 114
R. temporaria temporaria 114
Ranatra linearis 137
Ranunculus aquatilis 60
R. flammula 50
R. lingua 50
R.l. 'Grandiflora' 50
Red Pest 139
Reedmace 52
Rheum palmatum 76
R.p. 'Bowles Crimson' 76
R.p. tanguticum 76
Rhodeus sericeus amarus 98
Rhopalosiphum nymphaeae 133
Riccia fluitans 96
Rice Fish 106
Roach 103
Rodgersia aesculifolia 76
R. pinnata 76
R. tabularis 76
Rudd 104
Rutilus rutilus 103

Sagittaria japonica 50, 51
S.j. 'Flore Pleno' 51
S. latifolia 51
S. sagittifolia 51
S. subulata 96
St Bernard's Lily 65
St Bruno Lily 65
Salvinia auriculata 92
Saprolegnia 138
Saururus cernuus 51

Saxifraga peltata 72
Scardinius erythrophthalmus 104
Schizostylis coccinea 77
S.c. 'Grandiflora' 77
S.c. 'Mrs Hegarty' 77
Scirpus 'Albescens' 51
S. lacustris 51, 52
S. tabernaemontani 51, 52
S.t. 'Zebrinus' 43, 51
Sedge: Pendulous 45; Pond 45
Shubunkin 100; Bristol Blue 99;
    Cambridge Blue 99
Silurus glanis 105
Slime Disease 139
Snails: Ear Pond 113; Great Pond
    112; Ramshorn 113; Wandering
    Pond 113
Spanish Terrapin 116
·*Sparganium ramosum* 52
Spawn Binding 142
Spearwort: Greater 50; Lesser 50
Starfruit 45
Starwort Autumnal 57
Stonewort 57
Stratiotes aloides 61, 62
Stream 64
Struthiopteris germanica 77
Sunfish 106
Swamp Aster 65
Swamp Milkweed 65
Sweet Flag 42
Sweet Galingale 45
Symplocarpus foetidus 77

Tail Rot 138
Tench: Golden 105; Green 105
Thalia dealbata 92
Thrumwort 45
Tillaea recurva 61
Tinca tinca 105
Toad, Common 115
Trapa natans 62
Triturus cristatus cristatus 115
T. helveticus helveticus 115
T. vulgaris vulgaris 115
Trollius asiaticus 77
T. 'Canary Bird' 77
T. europaeus 77
T. 'Fire Globe' 77
T. 'Orange Princess' 77
Typha angustifolia 52
T. laxmannii 52
T. minima 52
T. stenophylla 52

Umbrella Grass 45
Unio pictorum 98, 113
Utricularia intermedia 62
U. minor 62
U. vulgaris 62

Index

Vallisneria spiralis 96
V.s. 'Torta' 96
Variegated Water Grass 46
Veronica beccabunga 57
Victoria amazonica 3

Waller 105
Wasting 143
Water: Aspidistra 93; Boatman 137;
   Celery 57; Chestnut 62; Chinkapin
   90; Clover 95; Crowfoot 60;
   Dropwort 60; Forget-me-not 20,
   49; Fringe 40; Hyacinth 91;
   Plantain 43; Poppy 92; Scorpion
   137; Soldier 61, 62; Stargrass 95;
   Stick Insect 137; Trumpet 94;
   Violet 59
Waterfalls 6-10
Water Garden: Siting 3; Concrete 17,
   125
Waterlilies: Planting 21-6; Propaga-
tion 27, 81
Waterlily: 'Blue Pygmy' 83; 'Cape
   Blue' 83; 'Cape Cod' 30; 'Common
   White' 29; 'Daubeny's' 84; Frog
   83; Magnolia 31; Mill Pond 30;
   'Pgymy White' 31; 'Red Indian' 86;
   'Royal Blue' 83; 'Sweet Scented'
   30
Waterlily pests and diseases: Aphis
   133; Beetle 133; Leaf Spot 134;
   Root Rot 134
Wels 105
White Spot Disease 140, 141
Willow Moss 58
Woodwardia virginica 78

Yellow Flag 47

Zantedeschia aethiopica 92
Z.a. 'Crowborough' 93